MW01701748

UNDYING HOPE

Special Features

Lessons

Unit 1: The Kingdom of God

Unit 2: Resurrection Hope

Unit 3: A Call to Holy Living

Quarterly Quiz

Use these questions as a pretest or as a review. The answers are on page iv of This Quarter in the Word.

Lesson 1

1. Daniel had a ________ that included visions from God. *Daniel 7:1, 2*

2. Daniel saw "the Ancient of days" wearing a purple robe, the sign of royalty. T/F. *Daniel 7:9*

Lesson 2

1. In his confession, Daniel affirmed that God keeps His "covenant and _______." *Daniel 9:4*

2. The curse God sent on Israel was according to what? (Law of Moses, Psalms, Job?) *Daniel 9:11*

Lesson 3

1. While beside the Ulai River, Daniel was visited by an angel named _______. *Daniel 8:16*

2. In Daniel's vision, the king of Grecia (Greece) is represented by a goat. T/F. *Daniel 8:21*

Lesson 4

1. Luke's account of the last supper features two cups. T/F. *Luke 22:17-20*

2. At the last supper, there was dissension among the disciples regarding who was the traitor and who was the _______. *Luke 22:23, 24*

Lesson 5

1. Jesus noted what emotion in the disciples on the Emmaus road? (joy, fear, sadness?) *Luke 24:17*

2. The disciples in Emmaus never realized that they had been talking to Jesus. T/F. *Luke 24:31-33*

Lesson 6

1. The resurrected Jesus invited the disciples to inspect both His hands and feet. T/F. *Luke 24:39*

2. After the resurrection, Jesus ate a piece of what? (fish, bread, fruit?) *Luke 24:42, 43*

Lesson 7

1. People were amazed to hear the disciples speak in other tongues because the people knew that those speaking were from _____. *Acts 2:6, 7*

2. People from Cyprus are noted as having been present on the Day of Pentecost. T/F. *Acts 2:9-11*

Lesson 8

1. The Lord's return will be accompanied by the _____ of the archangel. *1 Thessalonians 4:16*

2. The return of Jesus is compared with that of a ______ in the night. *1 Thessalonians 5:2*

Lesson 9

1. Paul said that the Thessalonians had much to fear about the future. T/F. *2 Thessalonians 2:2*

2. Christ's return will be preceded by a "woman of sin." T/F. *2 Thessalonians 2:3*

Lesson 10

1. Peter notes that the prophets were inspired by the Spirit of Christ. T/F. *1 Peter 1:10, 11*

2. Peter tells his readers to gird up the loins of their what? (spirit, mind, soul?) *1 Peter 1:13*

Lesson 11

1. We are to be diligent in making our calling and _______ sure. *2 Peter 1:10*

2. The Old Testament prophets gave their best personal opinions about the Messiah who was to come. T/F. *2 Peter 1:20, 21*

Lesson 12

1. Since "the end of all things is at hand," we are to do what two things? (fast and tithe, preach and teach, be sober and watch?) *1 Peter 4:7*

2. Charity (love) covers a multitude of _______. *1 Peter 4:8*

Lesson 13

1. For the Lord, a day is like what? (a waterfall, a thousand years, a walled city?) *2 Peter 3:8*

2. When Christ comes again, the old heavens and earth will be destroyed by _______. *2 Peter 3:10-12*

QUARTER AT A GLANCE

by Mark S. Krause

DORIS DAY had a huge hit in the 1950s with the song, "Que Sera, Sera (Whatever Will Be, Will Be)." More than 50 years later, this song expresses a common viewpoint of the future: whatever is going to happen, is going to happen. We have no control over the future, nor do we have any clues as to what it might be like.

The Bible does not share this view, for it is a book of hope. The Bible's outlook of hope is that of faith based on evidence. We believe God, who raised Jesus from the dead. This faith gives us the assured hope of salvation. Our future may have hardships ahead, but we are sustained by this glorious hope: one day we will be with the Lord forever (1 Thessalonians 4:17, Lesson 8).

Unit 1: The Kingdom of God

This quarter's lessons look at some of the key passages of Scripture that contribute to the Bible's message of hope. From the Old Testament we will have three lessons from Daniel, a man of God who was given glorious visions of the future. Although both frightening and mysterious, these visions have a theme of hope running through them. It is a hope for a future day when God will vindicate and reward His people. Daniel's hope is not based on human goodness or accomplishment, but on the mighty works and faithfulness of the Lord God.

Unit 2: Resurrection Hope

Hundreds of years after Daniel's time, Jesus came to Jerusalem to celebrate the Passover for the final time (Lesson 4). A tumultuous week ended with His crucifixion on Friday and burial in a borrowed tomb. Hope seemed to have died as well.

Yet that was not the end, for on the first day of the week Jesus began to appear to His disciples after He had risen from the dead (Lessons 5 and 6). The resurrected Lord gave hope to the community of disciples, a hope that continued after Jesus ascended into Heaven.

Jesus' departure left the core group of disciples in Jerusalem, waiting for what was to come next. On the Day of Pentecost, they experienced the powerful arrival of the Holy Spirit (Lesson 7), one of the most dramatic events recorded in the Bible! The gospel message of hope was launched into the world on that day.

The first-century church taught not only that Jesus was risen, but also that He would come again. Many expected that that would happen within a few days, months, or perhaps years. When that expectation went unmet, the apostle Paul wrote two letters of reassurance to his friends in Thessalonica (Lessons 8 and 9). His reassurance included warnings that some of the events preceding Jesus' return would be distressing. But when Christ comes again, those who have placed faith in Him will forget all pain and hardship as evil is finally and completely overthrown by Jesus.

> ***One day we will be with the Lord forever.***

Unit 3: A Call to Holy Living

We will investigate the two letters written by the apostle Peter to wrap up this quarter's study of hope. Peter wrote nearly 40 years after Christ ascended into Heaven, and some scoffed at the idea that Jesus would return. Peter's assurance is that though the return of Jesus may seem to be delayed, He will surely come. The church has held this assured hope for nearly two millennia.

Today's Hope

Hope is essential to our well-being. We need to believe that currently painful circumstances will be better in the future. In Jesus they will be! The Christian's salvation is sure. We of all people have cause for hope.

GET THE SETTING

by Ronald L. Nickelson

HOPE IS OUR FOCUS for the quarter. Perhaps a good working definition of *hope* is that it is the ability to envision and expect a better future.

We see this human ability throughout the pages of the Bible. Indeed, if you count the expressions of hope (and lack of hope) in the Bible, you will find dozens and dozens of occurrences. But what did hope (and lack of hope) mean to God's people?

One way to enrich our understanding of biblical hope is to examine it against the backdrop of how the pagan world of antiquity understood this concept. We can look at the ancient pagan's concept of *hope* in terms of two broad categories: what people hoped for in this life, and what people hoped for in the next life. We will consider these two categories in reverse order.

Hope Regarding Life After Death

One would think that we should approach our two categories in chronological order: first, investigate how ancient pagans expressed hope for their lives in this world, then take a look at what they hoped for in the hereafter. But there is a very good reason to do it the other way around.

Ancient pagans often expressed a very bleak view of what human existence would be like after death. Because they had such a despairing view of the afterlife, they ended up with a very "this worldly" focus regarding hope. In other words, we are considering the pagan outlook on hope for the afterlife first because their dismal outlook in this regard forced them to look to this life as the primary place for any hope.

An influential figure in creating a bleak outlook on the afterlife was the Greek poet Homer (that's a sculpture of him on the right). He may have lived in the eighth century BC, about the time of biblical prophets such as Amos. In his famous work the *Odyssey,* Homer imagines Odysseus, king of Ithaca, taking a trip to the underworld, the abode of the dead. Odysseus finds this place (hades) to be one of misery.

In this underworld, Odysseus meets Achilles, a dead hero of the Trojan War. Achilles famously laments that he would rather be a slave to the lowest person among the living than to be king of all the dead of hades. Existence in this kind of afterlife was not something to be anticipated!

This wasn't the only pagan viewpoint, of course. Some philosophers proposed the possibility of a blissful afterlife, reincarnation, the rebirth of the earth after its destruction, etc. But these seem to have been minority viewpoints. One concept never considered in a positive light was that of *resurrection.* Acts 17:32 notes the scoffing of pagan philosophers when Paul mentioned this idea.

Hope in This Life

Since ancient pagans saw little to hope for in the hereafter, they tended to focus on what could be gained in this world. Greek mythology had a goddess of hope in this regard, named *Elpis.* The Roman equivalent was the goddess *Spes,* and the Romans built temples in her honor. The mythology behind Elpis/Spes is rather complicated. But the bottom line seems to be that human imagination created a goddess who could provide whatever humans hoped for.

These hopes included many things we value today, such as personal, family, and cultural stability. The most "enduring" thing a pagan could hope for was a good name, a good reputation that would outlive oneself. Perhaps Paul was reflecting on the emptiness of this viewpoint when he wrote, "If in this life only we have hope in Christ, we are of all men most miserable" (1 Corinthians 15:19). How great is the Christian's hope!

Photo: Photos.com / Thinkstock

Mon, May 13	**Trust God to Provide**	Luke 12:22-28
Tue, May 14	**The Unfailing Treasure**	Luke 12:29-34
Wed, May 15	**Be Alert and Ready**	Luke 12:35-40
Thu, May 16	**The Faithful and Prudent Manager**	Luke 12:41-48
Fri, May 17	**The Perfect Gift from Above**	James 1:12-18
Sat, May 18	**Faithful in Little and Much**	Luke 16:10-13
Sun, May 19	**Good Stewards of God's Grace**	1 Peter 4:1-11
Mon, May 20	**Distressing Times Will Come**	2 Timothy 3:1-9
Tue, May 21	**Warnings for False Prophets**	Jeremiah 23:23-32
Wed, May 22	**Warnings for Rich Oppressors**	James 5:1-6
Thu, May 23	**Return to the Lord**	Hosea 14:1-7
Fri, May 24	**Teaching the Ways of God**	Micah 4:1-5
Sat, May 25	**I Will Come Again**	John 14:1-7
Sun, May 26	**The Promise of the Lord's Coming**	2 Peter 3:3-15a, 18

Answers to the Quarterly Quiz on page 226

Lesson 1—1. dream. 2. false. **Lesson 2**—1. mercy. 2. Law of Moses. **Lesson 3**—1. Gabriel. 2. true. **Lesson 4**—1. true. 2. greatest. **Lesson 5**—1. sadness. 2. false. **Lesson 6**—1. true. 2. fish. **Lesson 7**—1. Galilee. 2. false. **Lesson 8**—1. voice. 2. thief. **Lesson 9**—1. false. 2. false. **Lesson 10**—1. true. 2. mind. **Lesson 11**—1. election. 2. false. **Lesson 12**—1. be sober and watch. 2. sins. **Lesson 13**—1. a thousand years. 2. fire or heat.

This Quarter in the Word

Mon, Feb. 25	**The Lord Deals with the Mighty**	Daniel 5:13-21
Tue, Feb. 26	**The Lord Judges the Powerful**	Daniel 5:22-31
Wed, Feb. 27	**The Plot to Undermine Daniel**	Daniel 6:1-10
Thu, Feb. 28	**The Plot Fails**	Daniel 6:11-23
Fri, Mar. 1	**Daniel's God Is Exalted**	Daniel 6:24-28
Sat, Mar. 2	**Daniel's Vision**	Daniel 7:1-8
Sun, Mar. 3	**The Exaltation of the Coming One**	Daniel 7:9-14
Mon, Mar. 4	**Daniel's Resolve**	Daniel 1:8-15
Tue, Mar. 5	**Daniel's Recognition**	Daniel 1:16-21
Wed, Mar. 6	**The King's Challenge**	Daniel 2:1-11
Thu, Mar. 7	**Daniel's Intervention**	Daniel 2:12-16
Fri, Mar. 8	**Daniel's Success**	Daniel 2:36-49
Sat, Mar. 9	**Daniel's Prayer of Supplication**	Daniel 9:15-19
Sun, Mar. 10	**Daniel's Prayer of Confession**	Daniel 9:4-14
Mon, Mar. 11	**A Helper in Response to Prayer**	Daniel 9:20-27
Tue, Mar. 12	**A Guide into the Future**	Exodus 23:20-25
Wed, Mar. 13	**A Messenger of Rebuke**	Judges 2:1-5
Thu, Mar. 14	**A Messenger with Good News**	Luke 1:8-20
Fri, Mar. 15	**A Messenger from God**	Luke 1:26-38
Sat, Mar. 16	**A Helper in Understanding**	Daniel 8:1, 13-18
Sun, Mar. 17	**A Helper in Facing the Future**	Daniel 8:19-26

Mon, Mar. 18	**Keeping the Passover to the Lord**	Deuteronomy 16:1-8
Tue, Mar. 19	**What Does This Observance Mean?**	Exodus 12:21-27
Wed, Mar. 20	**Preparations for the Last Supper**	Luke 22:7-13
Thu, Mar. 21	**Partaking of the Lord's Table**	1 Corinthians 10:14-22
Fri, Mar. 22	**Showing Contempt for the Church**	1 Corinthians 11:17-22
Sat, Mar. 23	**Examine Yourselves**	1 Corinthians 11:23-32
Sun, Mar. 24	**The Last Supper**	Luke 22:14-30
Mon, Mar. 25	**The Trial Before Pilate**	Luke 23:13-25
Tue, Mar. 26	**The Crucifixion of Jesus**	Luke 23:32-38
Wed, Mar. 27	**The Death of Jesus**	Luke 23:44-49
Thu, Mar. 28	**The Burial of Jesus**	Luke 23:50-56
Fri, Mar. 29	**The Messiah's Suffering**	Isaiah 53:3-9
Sat, Mar. 30	**Discovery of the Empty Tomb**	Luke 24:1-12
Sun, Mar. 31	**The Lord Has Risen Indeed!**	Luke 24:13-21, 28-35
Mon, Apr. 1	**Appearances of the Risen Lord**	1 Corinthians 15:1-8
Tue, Apr. 2	**The Appearance to Mary Magdalene**	John 20:11-18
Wed, Apr. 3	**The Appearance to Thomas**	John 20:24-29
Thu, Apr. 4	**The Appearance to Seven Disciples**	John 21:1-8
Fri, Apr. 5	**Breakfast with the Disciples**	John 21:9-14
Sat, Apr. 6	**Simon Peter Called to Follow**	John 21:15-19
Sun, Apr. 7	**You Are Witnesses of These Things**	Luke 24:36-53
Mon, Apr. 8	**I Will Not Leave You Orphaned**	John 14:18-24
Tue, Apr. 9	**Abide in Me**	John 15:1-7
Wed, Apr. 10	**The Coming of the Comforter**	John 16:1-11
Thu, Apr. 11	**The Promise of the Spirit**	Acts 2:17-21
Fri, Apr. 12	**Raised Up and Freed from Death**	Acts 2:22-28
Sat, Apr. 13	**Both Lord and Christ**	Acts 2:29-36
Sun, Apr. 14	**The Day of Pentecost**	Acts 2:1-16

Mon, Apr. 15	**The Hopeless Human Situation**	Isaiah 59:9-15a
Tue, Apr. 16	**The Source of Hope**	Isaiah 59:15b-21
Wed, Apr. 17	**Waiting in Hope**	Psalm 38:9-15
Thu, Apr. 18	**Hoping Against Hope**	Romans 4:16-25
Fri, Apr. 19	**Seizing the Hope Set Before Us**	Hebrews 6:13-20
Sat, Apr. 20	**The God of Hope**	Romans 15:7-13
Sun, Apr. 21	**Encourage One Another with Hope**	1 Thessalonians 4:13–5:11
Mon, Apr. 22	**An Appointed Time**	Psalm 75
Tue, Apr. 23	**The Day Is Coming**	Malachi 4
Wed, Apr. 24	**No Good Thing Withheld**	Psalm 84
Thu, Apr. 25	**My Help Comes from the Lord**	Psalm 121
Fri, Apr. 26	**The Hope of Eternal Life**	Titus 3:1-7
Sat, Apr. 27	**Kept Sound and Blameless**	1 Thessalonians 5:23-28
Sun, Apr. 28	**Eternal Comfort and Good Hope**	2 Thessalonians 2:1-4, 8-17
Mon, Apr. 29	**I Have No Help in Me**	Job 6:8-13
Tue, Apr. 30	**Days Without Hope**	Job 7:1-6
Wed, May 1	**Will Mortals Live Again?**	Job 14:7-17
Thu, May 2	**My Times Are in Your Hands**	Psalm 31:9-16
Fri, May 3	**The Lord Preserves the Faithful**	Psalm 31:19-24
Sat, May 4	**Hope in God's Faithfulness**	Lamentations 3:19-24
Sun, May 5	**New Birth into a Living Hope**	1 Peter 1:3-16
Mon, May 6	**Full of Goodness and Knowledge**	Romans 15:14-21
Tue, May 7	**The Beginning of Knowledge**	Proverbs 1:2-7
Wed, May 8	**An Example in Self-Control**	Titus 1:5-9
Thu, May 9	**Enduring to the End**	Matthew 24:9-14
Fri, May 10	**A Life of Godliness and Dignity**	1 Timothy 2:1-7
Sat, May 11	**Love for One Another**	1 Peter 3:8-12
Sun, May 12	**Standing on God's Precious Promises**	2 Peter 1:2-15, 20, 21

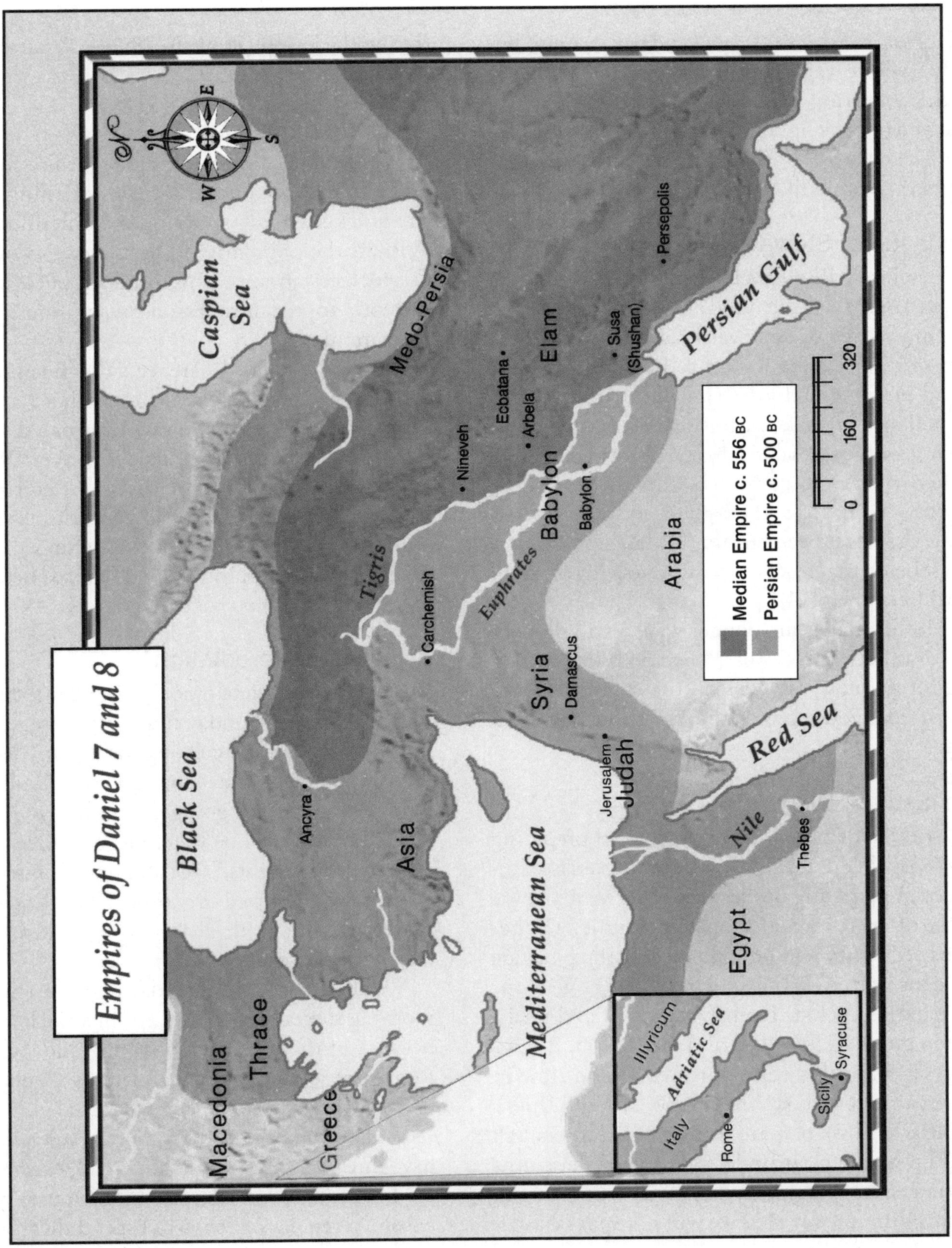
Empires of Daniel 7 and 8
Black Sea
Caspian Sea
Medo-Persia
Elam
Ecbatana
Arbela
Nineveh
Susa (Shushan)
Persepolis
Persian Gulf
Tigris
Euphrates
Babylon
Babylon
Carchemish
Arabia
Syria
Damascus
Jerusalem
Judah
Red Sea
Nile
Thebes
Egypt
Ancyra
Asia
Mediterranean Sea
Macedonia
Thrace
Greece
Illyricum
Adriatic Sea
Italy
Rome
Sicily
Syracuse
Median Empire c. 556 BC
Persian Empire c. 500 BC
0
160
320
N
E
S
W

YOUR SEVEN DAYS

Teacher Tips by Brent L. Amato

YOU MUST TEACH on Sunday morning, but you've waited until Saturday night to begin preparing your lesson. Now time is short, and you're stuck on something. "I had seven days," you say to yourself. "Why did I put off preparing?" Does this sound like you?

An Issue of Stewardship

Teaching, like other activities of life, is an opportunity to glorify God (1 Corinthians 10:31). We are to be good stewards of how we use the gift of teaching, as we are to be good stewards of all our spiritual gifts (1 Peter 4:10). Each of us will give an account to the master teacher for each lesson that we teach (2 Corinthians 5:10). When that time comes, I want to hear those words, "Well done, thou good and faithful servant: thou hast been faithful" (Matthew 25:21). I am sobered that teachers are held to a higher standard (see James 3:1).

All this makes me ponder what I will do with the time between lessons. When do I start preparing for the next Bible lesson that I am to teach? What does good stewardship say about my seven days?

An Issue of Diligence

As Luke demonstrated diligence in preparing his Gospel (Luke 1:3, 4), we are to exercise diligence in preparing our lessons. Will we make the most of every preparation opportunity (Ephesians 5:15, 16)? Will our preparation time include diligent prayer (1 Thessalonians 5:17)? Will our preparation include intensive study of and meditation on God's Word (Psalm 1:2; 119:15; 2 Timothy 2:15)? Will we use our preparation time in an organized and orderly manner (1 Corinthians 14:40)? Will we prepare so that our learners will end up with a clear understanding of the truths of the lesson (Nehemiah 8:8)? Will we prepare in such a diligent way that we will not speak hastily during the lesson (Proverbs 29:20)? What will we do with our seven days?

An Issue of Quality

We live in a culture of instant gratification and quick fixes. The quicker we get one thing done, the quicker we can move on to something else. Witness the popularity of microwave ovens and fast-food restaurants. This mind-set can leak over into our approach to lesson preparation if we're not careful.

Think about the difference. Would you rather eat a prepackaged frozen dinner that has been zapped quickly in a microwave oven or a dish that has simmered all day in a slow cooker? Would you rather drink "instant" coffee or coffee that has been brewed slowly? Will your learners prefer "instant" spiritual food that was whipped up on Saturday night or spiritual food that has been prepared over the course of seven days?

An Issue of Percolation

Starting your preparation on Sunday afternoon for the following Sunday morning's lesson results in a process I call "percolating the lesson." Starting preparation on Sunday afternoon will result in an awareness of things going on around you. Over seven days you will be watching and listening for God to drop insights, large and small. Lessons are refined and improved over time. New ideas occur; material is focused, changed, even discarded; creativity blossoms!

We all know that a Saturday night or a Sunday morning sometimes "blows up" in a teacher's face because of the unexpected stuff of life. Starting to prepare sooner rather than later is a wonderful hedge against such challenges.

When I come home from church each Sunday, I have three options: (1) take a nap, (2) watch sports on TV, or (3) spend a few minutes on next week's lesson. Seven days. How will I spend them?

Daniel's Vision of Change

Devotional Reading: Daniel 6:25-28
Background Scripture: Daniel 7

Daniel 7:1-3, 9-14

1 In the first year of Belshazzar king of Babylon Daniel had a dream and visions of his head upon his bed: then he wrote the dream, and told the sum of the matters.

2 Daniel spake and said, I saw in my vision by night, and, behold, the four winds of the heaven strove upon the great sea.

3 And four great beasts came up from the sea, diverse one from another.

. . . .

9 I beheld till the thrones were cast down, and the Ancient of days did sit, whose garment was white as snow, and the hair of his head like the pure wool: his throne was like the fiery flame, and his wheels as burning fire.

10 A fiery stream issued and came forth from before him: thousand thousands ministered unto him, and ten thousand times ten thousand stood before him: the judgment was set, and the books were opened.

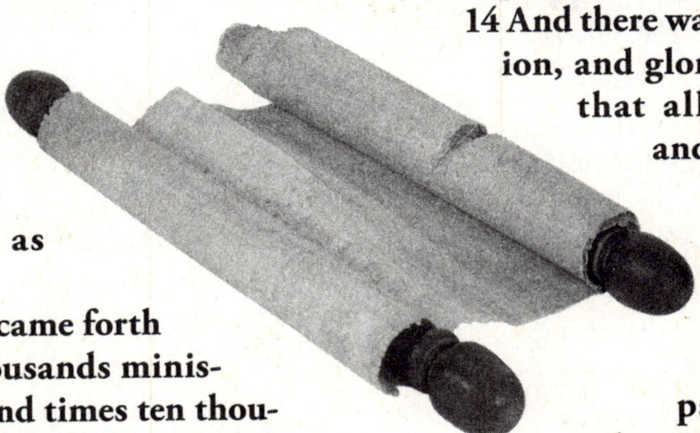

11 I beheld then because of the voice of the great words which the horn spake: I beheld even till the beast was slain, and his body destroyed, and given to the burning flame.

12 As concerning the rest of the beasts, they had their dominion taken away: yet their lives were prolonged for a season and time.

13 I saw in the night visions, and, behold, one like the Son of man came with the clouds of heaven, and came to the Ancient of days, and they brought him near before him.

14 And there was given him dominion, and glory, and a kingdom, that all people, nations, and languages, should serve him: his dominion is an everlasting dominion, which shall not pass away, and his kingdom that which shall not be destroyed.

Key Verse

There was given him dominion, and glory, and a kingdom, that all people, nations, and languages, should serve him: his dominion is an everlasting dominion, which shall not pass away, and his kingdom that which shall not be destroyed. —**Daniel 7:14**

Photo: Hemera Technologies / PhotoObjects.net / Thinkstock

UNDYING HOPE

Unit 1: The Kingdom of God

LESSONS 1–3

LESSON AIMS

After participating in this lesson, each student will be able to:

1. Recall the elements of Daniel's dream.
2. Explain why Daniel's dream was important for his day and is important for ours.
3. List reasons why Daniel's dream is a source of comfort to him or her.

LESSON OUTLINE

Introduction
- A. That's Just the Way It Is
- B. Lesson Background

I. Vision Begins (DANIEL 7:1-3)
- A. Dream Recorded (v. 1)
  - *"I Saw Jesus in the Kitchen"*
- B. Seas Stirred (v. 2)
- C. Beasts Emerge (v. 3)

II. Ancient of Days Enthroned (DANIEL 7:9, 10)
- A. Thrones Set (v. 9)
- B. Books Opened (v. 10)
  - *What Is a Book?*

III. Beasts Defeated (DANIEL 7:11, 12)
- A. One Slain (v. 11)
- B. Others Deposed (v. 12)

IV. Son of Man Appears (DANIEL 7:13, 14)
- A. Arrival (v. 13)
- B. Exaltation (v. 14)

Conclusion
- A. Ah, But Don't You Believe Them
- B. Prayer
- C. Thought to Remember

Introduction

A. That's Just the Way It Is

While millions of people struggle to feed their families, professional athletes receive millions to move a ball and score points in a televised game. While innovative thinkers with life-improving ideas cannot gain a public hearing, the masses tune in daily to hours of mindless entertainment media. While innocent people fear for their safety and livelihood, the wicked profit from the vulnerable and strut arrogantly without a care.

This is nothing new. The earliest humans observed the wicked thriving and the righteous barely surviving. Some will say, "Get over it—that's life." It is enough to make one cynical, to make us give up on the idea of a better world.

We can get stuck in mental ruts, and when we do, we need to be jarred out of this world's "reality" and into God's reality. We need Jesus to remind us again that the poor in spirit have the kingdom, the meek inherit the earth, the merciful receive mercy, the pure see God, and the peacemakers are considered His children (Matthew 5:3-9).

Long before Jesus issued that mountaintop reality check, the prophet Daniel opened the eyes of Jews in the sixth century BC so they could see what God was and would be doing. What Daniel saw was the ultimate triumph that God's followers today still long to see. It therefore has power to spare us the cynicism that can so easily ensnare.

B. Lesson Background

Daniel was one of the prominent Jews from Jerusalem who were taken to Babylon by King Nebuchadnezzar (Daniel 1:1-7). There were several deportations (compare Jeremiah 52:28). The fact that Daniel was taken in one of the early ones indicates that he was considered to be among the cream of the crop of the Israelite people.

During the exile, Daniel and other Jews struggled to understand what God was doing in the world. Why were the wicked Babylonians thriving while God's people, who were not nearly as wicked, suffered? Had God given up on the Jewish people? Did they have a future worth waiting for and praying for?

Some Jews conspired to take matters into their own hands (compare Jeremiah 41). They believed that the best way to push forward was to rebel against the Babylonians. They did not believe the prophesies of Habakkuk, Jeremiah, and others that God had decided to allow the Babylonians to triumph over the Israelites for their unfaithfulness. They did not comprehend that God would indeed punish the Babylonians for their own wickedness.

Other Jews gave up altogether. They stopped following Israel's God and turned to false gods. They assumed that if their God was the one true God, then they should always triumph over their enemies. To them, Babylon's victory over Israel was a victory of Babylon's gods over Israel's God (compare Jeremiah 44:18). Why worship a losing deity? So they transferred allegiance.

During times of such confusion, the Israelites needed a word from God to set the record straight. One such word came from Daniel.

I. Vision Begins

(Daniel 7:1-3)

A. Dream Recorded (v. 1)

1. In the first year of Belshazzar king of Babylon Daniel had a dream and visions of his head upon his bed: then he wrote the dream, and told the sum of the matters.

It is important to note which Babylonian king is reigning when Daniel has this dream. Two Babylonian kings are named in the book of Daniel: Nebuchadnezzar and Belshazzar. (Darius, a third king, is "the Median" by nationality in 5:31). Nebuchadnezzar reigned first, from about 605 to 562 BC. He was the one who destroyed Jerusalem and took many Jews into exile. The Babylonians seemed to realize that this was God's doing, but the Israelites did not (see Jeremiah 40:1-3).

Nebuchadnezzar is presented in Daniel as a king who has his own selfish agenda, but also as a king who is capable of respecting the true God (Daniel 4:34, 35). Belshazzar, who begins reigning about 553 BC, is presented less favorably. He is depicted as an arrogant king who mocks God by toying with the sacred Jerusalem temple vessels (5:2-4). God's response to such irreverence is not to humble Belshazzar as He did Nebuchadnezzar, but to bring him to deadly justice (5:18-30).

This is important because some world rulers whom God's people face after Daniel's day will be like Nebuchadnezzar, and others will be like Belshazzar. It is thus fitting that Daniel has his vision during the reign of Belshazzar, a vision about a future arrogant king whom God will bring to deadly justice.

HOW TO SAY IT

Babylon	*Bab*-uh-lun.
Babylonians	Bab-ih-*low*-nee-unz.
Belshazzar	Bel-*shazz*-er.
Habakkuk	Huh-*back*-kuk.
Medo-Persia	*Mee*-doe *Per*-zhuh.
Messiah	Meh-*sigh*-uh.
Nebuchadnezzar	*Neb*-yuh-kud-***nez***-er.
Zechariah	*Zek*-uh-***rye***-uh.

"I Saw Jesus in the Kitchen"

"Excuse me, I couldn't help noticing your shirt. Are you a priest?" I turned from browsing a jewelry display to see an older lady who had walked up. Surprised, I looked down and realized she had seen the Bible college logo on my T-shirt. She continued, "I need some advice. I saw Jesus in the kitchen last night. Do you think it means I'm going to die?" I confess my first thoughts were that she was mentally unbalanced or maybe had had a little too much to drink. But what if she really did see Jesus?

In Daniel's day, many people claimed to have direct communication with God. Some did, and some didn't. Telling them apart wasn't always easy. The Bible warns that false prophets are recognized by their untrue predictions (Deuteronomy 18:21, 22), promoting other gods (Deuteronomy 13:1-4), and/or bearing bad spiritual fruit (Matthew 7:15-20). Clearly, two of these tests require a "wait and see" approach.

Was the jewelry store lady a false prophetess? I don't know. But sorting that out in this brief encounter was not as important as pointing her toward Christ. "I think if Jesus appeared to you He would tell you He loves you and wants to be your Lord," I said. "I'd be glad to talk with you about that if you're interested." She looked at me strangely, politely declined, and went off to search for another minister. I think she thought *I* was the one who was crazy. —A. W.

B. Seas Stirred (v. 2)

2. Daniel spake and said, I saw in my vision by night, and, behold, the four winds of the heaven strove upon the great sea.

The sea is a place of fear and dread in the ancient world. It is also a symbol of chaos. Ancient people think that the sea is controlled by destructive gods and ruled by fierce beasts. They think this way because the earliest sailors who set out to navigate the open waters often do not come back. So people assume that such sailors have fallen victim to the sea's wrath. People learn that it is much safer to stick close to the shore when sailing.

So when *the four winds of the heaven* struggle *upon the great sea* in Daniel's vision, the reader should expect that chaos is brewing (compare Revelation 7:1). Normally, the wind blows from one direction only. The fact that it here blows from all directions may mean that a fearsome whirlpool is forming.

What Do You Think?

How does the blustery imagery of Daniel's dream resonate with your own experience of a turbulent time?

Talking Points for Your Discussion

- A time of spiritual turmoil
- A time of family turmoil
- A time of governmental turmoil
- John 16:33

C. Beasts Emerge (v. 3)

3. And four great beasts came up from the sea, diverse one from another.

Out of this chaotic sea emerge *four great beasts,* which represent four kings or kingdoms of the earth according to verse 17 (not in today's text). These beasts are described in greater detail in verses 4-8 (also not in today's text). Some students identify these four beasts with the empires of Babylon, Medo-Persia, Greece, and Rome. Not all agree on this identification, however (see further discussion with verse 11, below).

What Do You Think?

Would it be useful to use images of animals, etc., to describe the governmental or spiritual powers that affect us today? Why, or why not?

Talking Points for Your Discussion

- Issue of respect (1 Peter 2:17)
- Cultural and cross-cultural contexts
- "A picture is worth a thousand words"

II. Ancient of Days Enthroned

(Daniel 7:9, 10)

A. Thrones Set (v. 9)

9. I beheld till the thrones were cast down, and the Ancient of days did sit, whose garment was white as snow, and the hair of his head like the pure wool: his throne was like the fiery flame, and his wheels as burning fire.

The judgment scene is set. Thrones are installed and the judge has taken his seat. *The Ancient of days* is God, the one who always was and always will be (Revelation 4:8, 9). Other divine throne-scenes in Scripture include 1 Kings 22:19-22; Isaiah 6:1-9; Matthew 19:28; and Revelation 4.

That the everlasting God is judge is crucial to this vision. As one who sees everything, God alone can give a completely accurate account of what is really going on in world history. From the perspective of many Jewish exiles, God has lost to the Babylonian gods, and God's people have no future.

But God is not controlled by what "appears to be." He is not carried along by the momentum of the day. His *hair . . . like the pure wool* testifies to His ancient perspective, the same head of hair and perspective that the exalted Christ is depicted with in Revelation 1:12-16. The garment that is *white as snow* testifies to His purity. He is not a crooked judge, but is the source of true justice (compare Mark 9:3).

Another key component in this verse is fire. Both the throne and its wheels are aflame. Yet like the burning bush that Moses saw (Exodus 3:2), the fire does not consume the throne or its occupant. Fire is an image of judgment in Scripture. Posi-

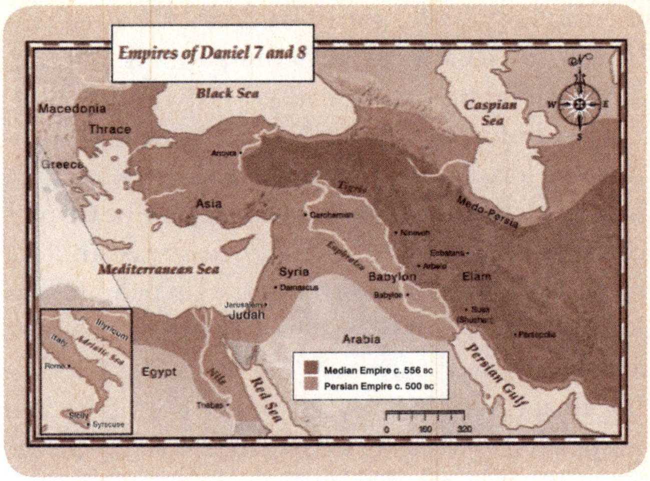

Visual for Lessons 1 & 3. *Keep this map posted as you study the lessons of Unit 1 to give your learners a geographical perspective.*

tively, fire can purify a precious metal like gold; in burning up the impurities, fire brings out true qualities (Zechariah 13:9; 1 Peter 1:7; Revelation 3:18). Fire consumes what does not last, incinerating what is worthless (compare 1 Corinthians 3:12-15). Fire is an instrument of eternal punishment (Deuteronomy 32:22; Matthew 5:22; 2 Peter 3:7).

B. Books Opened (v. 10)

10. A fiery stream issued and came forth from before him: thousand thousands ministered unto him, and ten thousand times ten thousand stood before him: the judgment was set, and the books were opened.

The fire that streams from God's presence likely indicates that He is about to judge. The thousands who surround Him are heavenly beings, or angels. Their vast number testifies to God's majesty as it does in Revelation 5:11. Daniel 5:1 tells us that Belshazzar has 1,000 nobles who feast in his presence. This impressive number is dwarfed by the multitude that waits on Israel's God. That these servants are present at this judgment scene also indicates that God has plenty of witnesses both to corroborate His judgment and to carry it out. What He decrees will certainly come to pass.

The books that are opened pertain to judgment. This passage does not specify whether they contain a list of misdeeds according to which the beasts will be judged or whether they indicate the names of those whom God spares judgment and therefore saves. Elsewhere in Scripture, the "book of life" appears to be an indication of who is saved (Psalm 69:28; Daniel 12:1; Revelation 3:5; 13:8; 17:8; 20:15; 21:27; 22:19). Revelation 20:12 is the strongest parallel to this passage. It is also a judgment scene in which multiple books are opened, including the book of life; persons are judged according to their works as listed in those books.

What Is a Book?

I read my first electronic book (or "e-book") just a few weeks ago. It's hard to wrap my mind around the concept that scrolling through a long document on a little computer counts as reading a book. Where are the pages? Where is the new (or old) book smell? How do I underline the good parts and find them again? But if we're feeling old, there are definite improvements: you can make the print larger with the push of a button, and if you still can't see it, then another button makes it read itself aloud!

When Daniel saw books opened in Heaven, he probably didn't see leather-bound tomes or computer monitors. Instead, he probably saw the scrolls or clay tablets familiar to his culture. Regardless of the format, the essence of a book is that of a permanent record.

Of course, God doesn't need the reminder of printed or digital pages as we might; His memory is perfect. But Daniel's vision serves as a warning to us that actions are recorded and that we will be called to account for them. Rather than trying to write the book of our life on our own, wouldn't it make sense to ask the author of life to help us write it?

—A. W.

III. Beasts Defeated

(Daniel 7:11, 12)

A. One Slain (v. 11)

11. I beheld then because of the voice of the great words which the horn spake: I beheld even till the beast was slain, and his body destroyed, and given to the burning flame.

The horn that is speaking belongs to the fourth, most terrifying beast (Daniel 7:7, 8). We learn more about this beast in verses 19-26. As mentioned above, some students identify this beast and its horns with the Roman Empire, although interpretations vary.

Our primary purpose, however, is not to identify this beast with a particular king or kingdom, but to focus on the kind of force this beast represents. Here we see audacity to speak and act against the one true God and His people. The impact of arrogant beasts (worldly rulers and their kingdoms) on the lives of God's people is felt during all ages. These beasts defy God Almighty and trample His people. King Belshazzar is neither the first nor the last to do this. Such beasts take many forms throughout history. If we are to resist their devouring ways, we must adopt God's view, which we get in the verses that follow.

What is most striking about the verse before us is what little effort God expends to strike this beast down. This beast is frighteningly powerful in the experience of those who suffer at its hands. Yet without fuss or fight, God simply slays the beast and burns its remains. When it comes to Israel's God, this beast is way out of its league. There cannot be a struggle, only instant defeat. God's people thus have no reason to fear even the most powerful humans. If God is for us, no one can stand against us (Romans 8:31).

What Do You Think?

When a situation turns out much differently from what most expect, how do we evaluate the presence or absence of God at work?

Talking Points for Your Discussion

- Political elections
- Healings
- Deliverance from danger
- Other

B. Others Deposed (v. 12)

12. As concerning the rest of the beasts, they had their dominion taken away: yet their lives were prolonged for a season and time.

By way of contrast, the other beasts receive considerably less judgment. Though it is true that they eventually lose control of their kingdoms, God allows them to retain control for a while.

This teaches us something about how God relates to the rulers and kingdoms of this world. All human institutions are fallen, and none is perfect. Their power is on loan from God (Romans 13:1). Some misuse that power so badly that God intervenes to bring them down. Other kings and kingdoms use their power in ways that God is willing to tolerate for a time. All human kingdoms ultimately will be replaced by God's kingdom. But some human kingdoms are better than others, and God relates to them in different ways.

What Do You Think?

Under what circumstances, if any, should a church "get involved in politics" to influence the course of a secular authority?

Talking Points for Your Discussion

- Regarding a biblical issue
- Regarding a non-biblical issue

IV. Son of Man Appears

(Daniel 7:13, 14)

A. Arrival (v. 13)

13. I saw in the night visions, and, behold, one like the Son of man came with the clouds of heaven, and came to the Ancient of days, and they brought him near before him.

Daniel's vision does not end only with bad news for those who rebel against God. It goes on to announce good news for those who are faithful.

This good news happens when *one like the Son of man* arrives. This designation has been interpreted in various ways. On the most basic level, the role that this being plays in the vision should be noticed. Previously, Daniel saw four beasts that looked "like" certain animals. Now he sees a being that looks *like the Son of man,* that is, like a human. In contrast with the beasts, this figure is humanlike. This is good news for God's people, who do not fare well under the rule of the beasts.

In Daniel 8:17, the phrase "son of man" is used to contrast a human with an angel. From an angel's perspective, "son of man" is another way of saying "descendant of Adam." But it makes no sense in this vision for God to exalt a mere human the way He is going to exalt this particular *one like the Son of man.* For the same reason, it makes no sense that this being would be an angel, such as Michael (Daniel 10:13, 21; 12:1). The ancient Jews never expect an angel to be given the kingdom (see Daniel 7:14, below).

Two positions remain. One asserts that the *Son of man* figure represents the people of Israel. This idea is drawn from Daniel 7:18, where God's people receive the kingdom. This makes sense in light of the biblical story, since God promises His people through the prophets that Israel is to be exalted above all nations. However, the New Testament is also very clear that Jesus identifies himself as this Son of man. In various places, He is the "Son of man" who is over "the kingdom" and whom people see "coming in the clouds" (Matthew 13:41-43; 16:28; 19:28; 24:30; 26:64).

We do not need to choose between these two options. Jesus is the one to whom God has given the kingdom, and God's people are the ones with whom Jesus shares His kingdom. For Jesus to receive the kingdom is thus for God's people to receive the kingdom as well. Since the ancient Jews expect a Messiah who will someday come and reign forever on David's throne, it is natural for them to identify this Son of man with that Messiah. We know that Messiah to be Jesus.

B. Exaltation (v. 14)

14. And there was given him dominion, and glory, and a kingdom, that all people, nations, and languages, should serve him: his dominion is an everlasting dominion, which shall not pass away, and his kingdom that which shall not be destroyed.

The fate of the Son of man is entirely different from that of the arrogant beast. The arrogant beast has dominion over many nations; the Son of man reigns over all nations and all people everywhere. The arrogant beast has power for a brief time; the Son of man rules forever. The arrogant beast is destroyed swiftly; the Son of man's kingdom *shall not be destroyed.*

The subjects of the Son of man therefore have nothing to fear. As long as they remain loyal to Him, they will share in a kingdom that *is an everlasting dominion.*

What Do You Think?

How does knowing that "God's people win in the end" affect the way you live right now? What changes do you need to make?

Talking Points for Your Discussion

- In lifestyle choices
- In speech patterns
- In relationships
- 2 Corinthians 4:16-18

Conclusion

A. Ah, But Don't You Believe Them

Note in today's Scriptures how world kingdoms end and how God's kingdom comes: God does it all. God's people do, however, have an important responsibility: to be God's heralds and witnesses (Matthew 28:19, 20). Our job is to tell the whole world that our king reigns, that His kingdom will never end, and that He has invited all people to become His subjects.

We must tell the world that while things appear bleak now, appearances can be deceiving. If anyone tells you, "That's just the way it is, some things will never change," don't believe them!

B. Prayer

We thank You, Lord, for giving us eyes to see. Though Daniel could only look forward to the coming kingdom, we can look back at its magnificent beginnings in Jesus. Yet we wait as Daniel waited, in anxious anticipation for the fullness of Your kingdom. Come, Lord Jesus; hasten that day. In Jesus' name, amen.

C. Thought to Remember

God's eternal kingdom surpasses all the fleeting kingdoms of this world.

VISUALS FOR THESE LESSONS

Involvement Learning

Some of the activities below are also found in the helpful student book, Adult Bible Class.
Don't forget to download the free reproducible page from www.standardlesson.com to enhance your lesson!

Into the Lesson

Sketch on the board the image of a person sleeping in bed; have two large "dream balloons" above his or her head. Ask, "What are some elements of a 'bad dream'?" Jot answers inside one of the dream balloons. *(Possible responses: presence of monsters, the dreamer is threatened by a powerful force or bad weather, etc.)*

Also ask, "What are some elements of a 'good dream'?" Jot ideas inside the other dream balloon. *(Possible responses: the dreamer is among friendly companions, an arriving hero "saves the day," the ending is happy and satisfying.)* After the discussion runs its course, say, "Today we're going to look at a dream recorded in the Bible. As we do, we may see some of these elements in that dream."

Alternative: Place in chairs copies of one or both of the activities from the reproducible page, which you can download. Learners can begin working on this as they arrive. *Option:* Divide learners into study groups of three to five people; have half of the groups work on one activity while the others work on the other activity. Discuss results, but do not let this segment drag out too long.

Into the Word

Distribute copies of the following True/False quiz, which you have titled "Daniel's Dream." Ask learners to pair off to work together.

Give these instructions: "Read Daniel 7:1-3, 9-14 and indicate if the following statements are true or false." 1. Daniel had a dream when Belshazzar was king of Persia. 2. Daniel's dream opened with a gentle breeze blowing over a calm ocean. 3. The four great beasts were different from one another. 4. Daniel saw the Ancient of Days standing in His glory. 5. The throne was "fiery" in some sense. 6. A stream of water flowed from the throne. 7. Books were opened. 8. A horn was speaking. 9. The body of a slain beast was thrown into the churning sea. 10. All four beasts were slain at the same time. 11. The "Ancient of days" came to the "Son of man." 12. The resulting kingdom is never destroyed. *(Answers: 1-F, v. 1; 2-F, v. 2; 3-T, v. 3; 4-F, v. 9; 5-T, v. 9; 6-F, v. 10; 7-T, v. 10; 8-T, v. 11; 9-F, v. 11; 10-F, v. 12; 11-F, v. 13; 12-T, v. 14.)*

There are various ways you can use this quiz. One option is first to read the text aloud, then have learners take the quiz with Bibles closed; results will indicate where further review is needed as your lesson progresses.

To give the key verse of Daniel 7:14 special attention, prepare handouts with the heading "Daniel 7:14, Key Verse Analysis." Space the following phrases randomly around the page:

And there was given him / dominion, and glory, / and a kingdom, / that all people, / nations, and languages, / should serve him: / his dominion is / an everlasting dominion / which shall not pass away, / and his kingdom / that which shall / not be destroyed.

Have these instructions at the top of the page: "Daniel 7:14 is a marvelous statement of what the "Son of man" of verse 13 is given. Draw lines to connect these phrases in the correct order without using your Bible." After learners finish, have the class read the key verse in unison with you several times.

Into Life

Say, "Daniel's dream is one that should comfort a child of God." Give each learner a sentence strip that reads, "Daniel says, 'Good night! Sleep tight!'" Once each learner has a strip, ask, "What is there about Daniel's dream that can enable you to have a 'good, sleep-tight' night?"

As the discussion winds down, suggest that each learner take his or her strip home and put it where it will be seen just before going to sleep each night in the week ahead. This will serve as a reminder of today's lesson.

Daniel's Prayer

Devotional Reading: James 5:13-18
Background Scripture: Daniel 9

Daniel 9:4-14, 17

4 And I prayed unto the Lord my God, and made my confession, and said, O Lord, the great and dreadful God, keeping the covenant and mercy to them that love him, and to them that keep his commandments;

5 We have sinned, and have committed iniquity, and have done wickedly, and have rebelled, even by departing from thy precepts and from thy judgments:

6 Neither have we hearkened unto thy servants the prophets, which spake in thy name to our kings, our princes, and our fathers, and to all the people of the land.

7 O Lord, righteousness belongeth unto thee, but unto us confusion of faces, as at this day; to the men of Judah, and to the inhabitants of Jerusalem, and unto all Israel, that are near, and that are far off, through all the countries whither thou hast driven them, because of their trespass that they have trespassed against thee.

8 O Lord, to us belongeth confusion of face, to our kings, to our princes, and to our fathers, because we have sinned against thee.

9 To the Lord our God belong mercies and forgivenesses, though we have rebelled against him;

10 Neither have we obeyed the voice of the Lord our God, to walk in his laws, which he set before us by his servants the prophets.

11 Yea, all Israel have transgressed thy law, even by departing, that they might not obey thy voice; therefore the curse is poured upon us, and the oath that is written in the law of Moses the servant of God, because we have sinned against him.

12 And he hath confirmed his words, which he spake against us, and against our judges that judged us, by bringing upon us a great evil: for under the whole heaven hath not been done as hath been done upon Jerusalem.

13 As it is written in the law of Moses, all this evil is come upon us: yet made we not our prayer before the Lord our God, that we might turn from our iniquities, and understand thy truth.

14 Therefore hath the Lord watched upon the evil, and brought it upon us: for the Lord our God is righteous in all his works which he doeth: for we obeyed not his voice.

. . . .

17 Now therefore, O our God, hear the prayer of thy servant, and his supplications, and cause thy face to shine upon thy sanctuary that is desolate, for the Lord's sake.

Key Verse

To the Lord our God belong mercies and forgivenesses, though we have rebelled against him. —**Daniel 9:9**

Undying Hope

Unit 1: The Kingdom of God

Lessons 1–3

Lesson Aims

After participating in this lesson, each student will be able to:

1. Summarize Daniel's prayer of confession.
2. Tell why confessing sin is important for groups (nations, etc.) as well as for individuals.
3. Write a prayer of confession for his or her own nation, community, or church.

Lesson Outline

Introduction

A. Confession and Apology

The terms *confession* and *apology* are an interesting pair. They are used most often in their negative senses, although each also has a positive sense. Negatively, to apologize is to say that one is sorry; positively, to offer an apology is to offer a defense of one's position (as in the word *apologetics*). In both instances, the focus is image management. We do not want people to think that our true identity is represented by a particular wrongdoing, and so we say we are sorry. We do not want them to think that a position we hold is flimsy, and so we offer an apology (or an apologetic) to convince them that it is intellectually respectable.

Confession in its negative sense is more intense than saying we are sorry; it means admitting that what we did was wrong. In so doing, we are affirming the existence of a moral order that is larger than ourselves and submitting our plea to the mercy of the one we have wronged. Confession in its positive sense is to affirm what we believe or the way things should be. To confess "Jesus is Lord" is to confess in a positive sense. We confess Christ because we are so convinced of His lordship and its implications for all creation that we cannot help but share this good news with everyone.

There is a time and place for both confession and apology. The sixth century BC of Daniel's day was a time for confession by the Jews.

B. Lesson Background

Daniel's prayer in today's text is best understood when viewed through a wide-angle lens. The national identity of the Israelites had its roots in God's promise to Abraham (who, ironically, was originally from Babylon) that he would become a great nation and that through him all nations would be blessed (Genesis 12:1-3).

An important element of this promise was God's deliverance of Abraham's descendants from slavery in Egypt (about 1440 BC), bringing them into the promised land. The people's well-being depended on their keeping God's law. Should the Israelites fail in that, God vowed to deliver them into their enemies' hands (Deuteronomy 28:15-68).

By Daniel's time many centuries later, that is exactly what had happened. The Israelites had forsaken God's ways, and God had kept His Word to judge them. Judgment was not, however, God's last word. He also foretold that should the Israelites return to Him wholeheartedly, then He would restore their fortunes (Deuteronomy 30:1-10). This is the most important background to Daniel's prayer in today's text.

Daniel offered his prayer in "the first year of Darius . . . which was made king over the realm of the Chaldeans" (Daniel 9:1). We date this to about 522 BC. Thus Daniel's prayer in today's text took place some 64 years after the destruction of the temple in Jerusalem. The rebuilding of the temple was started in 538 BC as the first wave of the Jews returned from exile (Ezra 1:1–4:5), but subsequently halted (4:24). The work on the temple resumed in 529 BC and was completed in 515 BC (5:1–6:15). Thus Daniel offered his prayer during a time of transition for his people. (Note: the Chaldeans are the same as the Babylonians.)

I. Confession

(Daniel 9:4-6)

A. God Approached (v. 4)

4. And I prayed unto the LORD my God, and made my confession, and said, O Lord, the great and dreadful God, keeping the covenant and mercy to them that love him, and to them that keep his commandments.

HOW TO SAY IT

apologetics	uh-*pah*-luh-***jeh***-tiks.
Assyria	Uh-*sear*-ee-uh.
Babylonian	Bab-ih-*low*-nee-un.
Chaldeans	Kal-*dee*-unz.
Constantine	***Kahns***-tun-*teen*.
Cyrus	*Sigh*-russ.
Darius	Duh-*rye*-us.
Lamentations	Lam-en-*tay*-shunz.
medieval	muh-*dee*-vul.
Nebuchadnezzar	*Neb*-yuh-kud-***nez***-er.
Theodosius	*Thee*-uh-***doe***-shus.
Wicca	*Wih*-kuh.

Daniel begins his prayer of confession by recognizing the great difference between God and His people. God is the one who is great. He is the one *keeping the covenant* while His people self-evidently do not. God's mercy is itself self-evident given the decree of Cyrus that already has been issued in the Jews' favor (Ezra 1). All the events to this point establish that God honors His Word and that His people forsake His commands. This difference is crucial for Daniel's request that we will see in verse 17, below. Since God is so different from His people, He may extend them mercy one more time.

Solomon used similar language of God in the dedication of the Jerusalem temple centuries earlier (1 Kings 8:23; 2 Chronicles 6:14). This is significant because Solomon's prayer anticipated the Israelites' eventual exile; in that light, his prayer beseeched God to remember them when they would cry out to Him. This is precisely what Daniel is doing. Several decades after Daniel's prayer, Nehemiah will describe God in nearly identical language. Nehemiah too will call on God to remember His people and restore them as they rebuild their city's walls (Nehemiah 1:5).

What Do You Think?

How is knowing God's character important for the way you pray? What adjustments do you need to make in this regard?

Talking Points for Your Discussion

- Exodus 33:13; 34:6, 7
- Nehemiah 9:19-23
- 2 Thessalonians 1:6
- Hebrews 4:15; 6:10; 12:29
- 1 John 1:5; 4:16

B. Precepts Rejected (v. 5)

5. We have sinned, and have committed iniquity, and have done wickedly, and have rebelled, even by departing from thy precepts and from thy judgments.

God wants His people to admit that they are responsible for their own demise. He wants them to recognize that disaster follows from sin. He wants them to become the type of people who do not repeat the same sinful mistakes, but grow in their knowledge of God and His requirements.

Daniel uses several expressions of confession in this light. The last expression in his list is perhaps the most noteworthy: the Israelites' sin has been the deliberate rejection of God's specific requirements (*thy precepts* and *thy judgments*). By naming the source of the problem, Daniel implies the path to recovery: the requirements of God that the people have left behind must be embraced anew.

What Do You Think?

When is confession of specific sins better than a general "I have fallen short" confession? When is a general confession more appropriate?

Talking Points for Your Discussion

- Leviticus 5:5
- Matthew 3:6
- Acts 19:18
- James 5:16
- 1 John 1:9

C. Messengers Ignored (v. 6)

6. Neither have we hearkened unto thy servants the prophets, which spake in thy name to our kings, our princes, and our fathers, and to all the people of the land.

God did not simply give His law to Moses, retreat to Heaven, wait for His people to violate it, and then judge them when they did. Out of compassion, He sent prophets time and again as they strayed. He did all He could to bring things under control. He sent these servants not just to those in charge, but to all the people. God had given the Israelites plenty of chances to rethink their unfaithfulness and get their lives in conformity with His will before things fell apart completely.

When the Innocent Confess

I have a friend who practices Wicca, a modern form of witchcraft. "Jill" turned to witchcraft in part because of abusive experiences in churches. Over the years, she has accumulated a whole litany of grievances against Christians, from the strangers who have criticized her for wearing a pentacle, to the church leaders of medieval and colonial eras who tortured accused witches in the name of God.

After several conversations regarding this, I wrote a sincere apology to Jill for the suffering she and similar people have experienced by misguided Christians. Although we both knew that I had never personally hurt her in these ways, taking this step let her know I empathized with her. This advanced both our friendship and her receptivity to the gospel.

Daniel confessed the sins of past generations of his people although he was personally innocent of those sins. His confession showed that he identified with God's outrage over Israel's behavior and wished that he could do something to change the situation. This placed him—and can place us—on God's side, ready to be used by Him to influence others. —A. W.

II. Realization

(Daniel 9:7-14)

A. Sharp Contrasts (vv. 7-11a)

7, 8. O Lord, righteousness belongeth unto thee, but unto us confusion of faces, as at this day; to the men of Judah, and to the inhabitants of Jerusalem, and unto all Israel, that are near, and that are far off, through all the countries whither thou hast driven them, because of their trespass that they have trespassed against thee. O Lord, to us belongeth confusion of face, to our kings, to our princes, and to our fathers, because we have sinned against thee.

Daniel continues to contrast God with His people. God is the one who is entirely in the right. He has done nothing wrong in judging His people as He has. He has made the terms of His covenant clear. He has established the consequences of rebellion. He has sent prophets to clarify the meaning of His covenant. He had warned that judgment was coming, giving plenty of opportunities to repent. Every step of the way, God has kept His word.

All this has left the Israelites entirely without excuse. The result is scandal or, as the *King James Version* translates it literally, *confusion of face*. The people are entirely responsible, and Daniel lets no one off the hook. Daniel faults not only the residents of Jerusalem and Judah, but all Israelites everywhere. Both those who stayed put in the land and those who have been scattered share the blame because all sinned against the Lord's commands. Powerful leaders are to blame (Jeremiah 44:17), as well as the average head of household (44:19).

9. To the Lord our God belong mercies and forgivenesses, though we have rebelled against him.

Daniel also knows that divine righteousness is not the only factor. God has also revealed himself to be a God of *mercies and forgiveness.* The Israelites have rebelled against God many times: by worshipping a golden calf (Exodus 32), by fearing the inhabitants of the promised land (Numbers 13), etc. Yet time and again, God worked through the sinful choices of His people, offering a way forward to His ultimate purposes for them. Daniel knows this about God.

What Do You Think?

How can you express gratitude for God's mercy today in ways other than prayer?

Talking Points for Your Discussion

- In interactions with fellow Christians
- In interactions with non-Christians
- In financial priorities
- In entertainment choices
- Other

10, 11a. Neither have we obeyed the voice of the Lord our God, to walk in his laws, which he set before us by his servants the prophets. Yea, all Israel have transgressed thy law, even by departing, that they might not obey thy voice.

After declaring God's mercy in verse 9, one might expect Daniel to conclude his prayer. He does not do so, however, because he is not after cheap forgiveness. Instead he continues to rehearse Israel's guilt.

It is worth remembering at this point why God sent prophets to urge His people *to walk in his laws:* God relentlessly pursues His people, not because they are special in and of themselves, but because He has called them to an important mission. They must walk in God's ways so the nations will see those ways and be drawn to God (Deuteronomy 4:5-8).

God is faithful when His people are faithless because God loves the whole world. His plan for saving this world involves forming a people to be His witnesses. The Israelites are not called to save the world; only God can do that. Yet even imperfect people can be used as witnesses to God. Why would the nations believe the witness of God's people if those people merely live like everyone else? They have to *be* different if they are going to *make* a difference. God knows that the credibility of His witnesses is crucial to the world's acceptance of their witness.

B. Sobering Results (vv. 11b-14)

11b. Therefore the curse is poured upon us, and the oath that is written in the law of Moses the servant of God, because we have sinned against him.

The curse of God that results should not be a surprise since a series of curses is presented in detail in Deuteronomy 28:15-68. All of the consequences listed there have come to pass. At the hands of Assyria, Babylon, and the smaller nations around Israel, God had brought judgment on His people in various ways through the centuries.

12. And he hath confirmed his words, which he spake against us, and against our judges that judged us, by bringing upon us a great evil: for under the whole heaven hath not been done as hath been done upon Jerusalem.

Daniel affirms his conviction that God is the one who has brought disaster on Israel. This conviction is itself an act of faith because not all Jews believe that God is the one who leveled Jerusalem and scattered His people. Some interpret these events as a sign of God's defeat. They think pagan gods have prevailed (see Jeremiah 44:17, 18). But Daniel has eyes to see God's hand at work.

This does not mean, however, that believers today are justified in attributing to God all the personal disasters that befall them. The Bible does not teach that all disaster comes from God. Even so, the Bible does affirm that God is capable of using all of our experiences to accomplish some good for us (Romans 8:28).

Visual for Lesson 2. *As you discuss verse 17, point to this visual and ask, "What are some barriers that would cause God not to hear our prayers, if any?"*

The Surprising Course of History

Rome built one of the greatest empires in history. The result was a uniting of the Mediterranean world with roads and aqueducts, an advanced legal system, and prosperous trade. At the same time, the Romans promoted idol worship, sexual immorality, slavery, and the torture of Christians. The demise of the Roman Empire clearly seems to have been a judgment of God (compare Revelation 17, 18).

There's a problem, though: Rome's final collapse did not come until *after* the empire had become Christianized! Constantine issued an edict of tolerance in AD 312, and Theodosius proclaimed Christianity the state religion in 380. These two emperors and others who followed worked vigorously to build churches, abolish immoral practices, promote doctrinal unity, and spread the faith to other lands. Yet within a few generations, barbarians had overrun their empire.

What's the explanation? Maybe they were false converts, just using Christianity for political ends. Maybe they were sincere, but it was simply too late. Or perhaps God knew that the migration of European tribes into Roman territory was the best way for new people groups to hear the gospel.

We cannot always pinpoint the reasons why nations rise and decline. Some of the least Christian nations in the world today are also among the most prosperous (examples: Saudi Arabia, Japan), while some predominantly Christian societies suffer abject poverty (example: Sub-Saharan Africa). God's purpose in working with the nations is so that people should reach out to Him and find Him (Acts 17:26, 27). Our part is to point people to Him and wait patiently as the surprising course of history unfolds. —A. W.

13, 14. As it is written in the law of Moses, all this evil is come upon us: yet made we not our prayer before the LORD our God, that we might turn from our iniquities, and understand thy truth. Therefore hath the Lord watched upon the evil, and brought it upon us: for the LORD our God is righteous in all his works which he doeth: for we obeyed not his voice.

Although Daniel continues to confess God's righteousness in bringing disaster on the Israelites, he further recognizes that there was a time when Israel could have averted it. Not only could the people have averted God's judgment by not sinning to begin with, they also could have averted it by reversing course once they had started sinning.

Notice in these verses that the Israelites need to do more than apologize for letting God down. When God's people sin, they need to turn from their sinful ways. Only in turning from sin do God's people show that they understand God's truth. God's truth is not simply an abstract set of intellectual principles to affirm or deny. Understanding God's truth means embracing the life to which God calls His people. This is made clearest in Jesus' claim to be the way, the truth, and the life (John 14:6). Confessing Jesus requires reordering our lives according to God's will. Anything short of this is a sham (see John 14:15).

What Do You Think?

What prayer burden is on your heart today? How have your prayer burdens changed as you have grown in spiritual maturity?

Talking Points for Your Discussion

- Prayers for yourself
- Prayers for fellow Christians
- Prayers for non-Christians
- Prayers for the church
- Other

III. Appeal
(Daniel 9:17)

A. To Hear (v. 17a)

17a. Now therefore, O our God, hear the prayer of thy servant, and his supplications.

Daniel 9:15, 16 (not in today's text) continues the contrast between the nature of God and the sin of the people. With verse 17 Daniel begins his appeal. The final verse of our study is not the final verse of Daniel's prayer, since it does not end until verse 19. Verse 17 nonetheless captures the substance of verses 17-19. Daniel wants God to act, but Daniel realizes that God must first be willing to hear prayers (compare Lamentations 3:44).

What Do You Think?

In the four-step prayer formula *Adoration, Confession, Thanksgiving, Supplication* (ACTS), where do you need to make the most improvement? How will you do so?

Talking Points for Your Discussion

- Elements of the Lord's prayer (Matthew 6:9-13)
- Prayer environment (Matthew 14:23)
- The issue of doubt (James 1:6)
- The issue of motives (James 4:3)
- Other

B. To Shine (v. 17b)

17b. And cause thy face to shine upon thy sanctuary that is desolate, for the Lord's sake.

As Daniel brings his petition to a close, he bases his appeal on the Lord's own sake, not on the sake of the people. Israel's disaster means that God's name—which is attached to His people, His city of Jerusalem, His sanctuary (temple)—has been profaned among the nations (compare Ezekiel 36:21-23), His reputation tarnished.

Of course, God is not insecure about what the nations think of Him. They have misconstrued who He is for a long time. He is concerned, however, with how the nations understand His unique relationship with His people. This is because His strategy for drawing all humans to himself involves the witness of His people. Although it is important that God discipline His people when their transgressions compromise His mission, to wipe them out altogether would also compromise that mission. God does not mind being known as the God who disciplines those whom He loves, but He also wants to be known as the God of mercy. Indeed, that's how Daniel himself knows God (Daniel 9:9, 18). The mercy that God shows His people is the same mercy He intends to show the nations.

For this reason, Daniel appeals to God's larger purposes. Daniel is committed to those larger purposes. The partially rebuilt temple (see the Lesson Background) is still a disgrace. Daniel calls on God to remember His plan because Daniel wants to renew Israel's commitment to that plan.

Conclusion

A. Daniel's Example

Daniel's prayer is a model in teaching us what it means to confess sins with integrity. We do not simply apologize to God. We must reorient our lives around God's mission. We must be honest about our past and deliberate about our future.

Daniel's prayer is also a wonderful example of corporate solidarity. In a world where leaders may not even own up to personal failings, it is remarkable to see someone who identifies with the sins of his people, both in his own generation and in generations past. Daniel makes no distinction between his behavior and that of Israel as a whole. Yet we know Daniel was a moral exemplar among his people. He took bold steps to honor God when his own life was on the line (Daniel 1 and 6).

But Daniel's life did not revolve around himself. If his people were not right with God, then God's mission was at stake. When God's mission is in jeopardy, God's people have to join together, confess together, and turn to God together.

B. Prayer

Lord, we continually fall short. We confess that we have a lot of growing up (and owning up) to do. Help us keep the bigger picture of Your mission in view. In Jesus' name, amen.

C. Thought to Remember

Confess sin and return to God.

Involvement Learning

Some of the activities below are also found in the helpful student book, Adult Bible Class.
Don't forget to download the free reproducible page from www.standardlesson.com to enhance your lesson!

Into the Lesson

Write the names *Daniel, Nehemiah,* and *Solomon* on the board. Then ask three volunteers to stand up front and read 1 Kings 8:23; Daniel 9:4; Nehemiah 1:5, one passage each. The readers are not to reveal to the class the passages where the readings are found. Ask, "Who addressed God in each of these prayers?" as you point to the three names. Have the verses read again, if necessary.

After the three names are matched correctly, write on the board *1 Kings 8:22-53* (next to the name Solomon), *Daniel 9:4-19* (next to Daniel); and *Nehemiah 1:3-11* (next to Nehemiah). Then ask, "What is a common element across these three prayers?" Allow learners to check their Bibles for possibilities. More than one answer is possible, but in particular make sure your class sees *confession of sin* as the common element. If you think this segment will take too long (because the three passages are lengthy), you can simply point out this common element yourself in 1 Kings 8:47; Daniel 9:5, 6; and Nehemiah 1:6, 7. Say, "Let's take an in-depth look at Daniel's prayer."

Alternative: Place in chairs copies of the "Addressing God" activity from the reproducible page, which you can download. Learners can begin working on this as they arrive.

Into the Word

Say, "Prayer realizes who God is and who we are in relationship to and comparison with Him. When we understand His power and love and see our own weaknesses, asking for His help is the appropriate thing to do."

Read aloud today's text, Daniel 4:4-14, 17. Then say, "In his prayer Daniel seems to be answering the unstated question, 'Who is God?' What are some of the answers he comes up with?" Divide learners into groups of four to six to develop a list of answers. Suggest that learners look at verses 1-3 as well as the lesson text.

Ask groups to share their suggestions with the class as a whole. Expect suggestions to include (1) God is merciful (v. 4), (2) God expects obedience (v. 4), (3) God is righteous (v. 7), (4) God is forgiving and gracious (v. 9), (5) God punishes sin and disobedience (vv. 11, 12, 14), (6) God can answer prayers (v. 17). Other suggestions are possible.

Then ask, "What is the appropriate response we should have to God as we have seen Him described thus far?" Some expected responses are that we come to Him (1) as sinners, those who have done wrong (v. 5), (2) as rebellious people (vv. 5, 9), (3) as those who have rejected His commands and laws (v. 5), (4) as people who have refused to listen to those He sends with His Word (v. 6), (5) confused and ashamed (vv. 7, 8), (6) as unfaithful (v. 7), (7) with grateful awareness of His mercies and forgiveness (v. 9), (8) with sins that need to be forgiven (v. 11), (9) in anticipation that our prayers will be heard (v. 17). Your learners may, of course, see other possibilities.

As you work through the text from Daniel's viewpoint and how that viewpoint speaks to our own prayer lives, be sure to address the concept of confessing the sins of past generations. Naturally, the one doing the praying is innocent in such cases. You may find the illustration "When the Innocent Confess" on page 244 helpful in this regard.

Option: If time allows, supplement this section of the lesson with the "An Attitude of Prayer" activity on the reproducible page, which you can download.

Into Life

Say, "It's time to stop talking about praying and pray." Allow time for brief prayer responses as you suggest categories for prayer from today's text. You can encourage silent praying or ask volunteers to pray aloud. Use "we statements" from today's text as prayer stimuli, adjusting them as necessary for today's context.

March 17
Lesson 3

Gabriel Interprets Daniel's Vision

Devotional Reading: Psalm 91:1-12
Background Scripture: Daniel 8

Daniel 8:1, 15-26

1 In the third year of the reign of king Belshazzar a vision appeared unto me, even unto me Daniel, after that which appeared unto me at the first.

. . . .

15 And it came to pass, when I, even I Daniel, had seen the vision, and sought for the meaning, then, behold, there stood before me as the appearance of a man.

16 And I heard a man's voice between the banks of Ulai, which called, and said, Gabriel, make this man to understand the vision.

17 So he came near where I stood: and when he came, I was afraid, and fell upon my face: but he said unto me, Understand, O son of man: for at the time of the end shall be the vision.

18 Now as he was speaking with me, I was in a deep sleep on my face toward the ground: but he touched me, and set me upright.

19 And he said, Behold, I will make thee know what shall be in the last end of the indignation: for at the time appointed the end shall be.

20 The ram which thou sawest having two horns are the kings of Media and Persia.

21 And the rough goat is the king of Grecia: and the great horn that is between his eyes is the first king.

22 Now that being broken, whereas four stood up for it, four kingdoms shall stand up out of the nation, but not in his power.

23 And in the latter time of their kingdom, when the transgressors are come to the full, a king of fierce countenance, and understanding dark sentences, shall stand up.

24 And his power shall be mighty, but not by his own power: and he shall destroy wonderfully, and shall prosper, and practise, and shall destroy the mighty and the holy people.

25 And through his policy also he shall cause craft to prosper in his hand; and he shall magnify himself in his heart, and by peace shall destroy many: he shall also stand up against the Prince of princes; but he shall be broken without hand.

26 And the vision of the evening and the morning which was told is true: wherefore shut thou up the vision; for it shall be for many days.

Key Verse

The vision of the evening and the morning which was told is true. —**Daniel 8:26a**

Photo: Jupiterimages / Photos.com / Thinkstock

Undying Hope

Unit 1: The Kingdom of God

Lessons 1–3

Lesson Aims

After participating in this lesson, each student will be able to:

1. Identify the ram, the goat, and the king of fierce countenance of Daniel's vision.
2. Trace the fulfillment of Daniel's vision.
3. Write a prayer that praises God for His sovereignty over human events.

Lesson Outline

Introduction
- A. Left Behind?
- B. Lesson Background

I. Meeting the Interpreter (Daniel 8:1, 15-19)
- A. Second Vision Is Received (v. 1)
- B. Gabriel Is Commissioned (vv. 15, 16)
- C. Daniel Is Resuscitated (vv. 17, 18)
- D. Interpretation Is Introduced (v. 19)
  - *Some Things Can't Be Rushed*

II. Receiving the Interpretation (Daniel 8: 20-26)
- A. Ram Is Identified (v. 20)
- B. Goat Is Identified (vv. 21, 22)
- C. Wicked King Is Judged (vv. 23-25)
- D. Vision Is Sealed (v. 26)
  - *Good Secrets*

Conclusion
- A. Apocalypse Now!
- B. Prayer
- C. Thought to Remember

Introduction

A. Left Behind?

Every once in a while a book series comes along that captures the imagination of millions of readers. What the Harry Potter series did for young people in the general public, the Left Behind series did for a broad range of Christian readers back around the turn of the millennium. That series is a imaginative account of the end of the world revolving around apocalyptic portions of Revelation. The events of Revelation are interpreted as if they were meant to give a literal play-by-play account of end-times tribulation.

This kind of interpretation draws a crowd partly because it plays off of the difficulty that readers have with apocalyptic texts such as the book of Revelation. The symbolic language of such texts is perplexing, and an interpreter who "connects the dots" in a way that seems fairly plausible can gain a wide hearing.

Daniel 8, today's lesson, is an apocalyptic text that can cause similar consternation since it involves key historical events represented symbolically by animals. This chapter is different from other apocalyptic texts, however, in that it also includes an angelic interpretation. We are not left guessing what the animals represent; we are told. Readers are led to understand better both the meaning of the animals in this chapter and the nature of *apocalypse* as a type of literature. This gives us clues for the proper reading of apocalyptic texts for which interpretations are not so obvious.

B. Lesson Background

Daniel 8 contains a vision of two animals and an interpretation of what they represent. The interpretation points to a future time long after the death of Daniel. Rather than focus on the Babylonian empire against which Daniel and the Jews of his time struggle, the vision focuses on the times of the Persians and Greeks that followed. A brief introduction to the Jewish encounter with these nations is therefore in order.

The Babylonians destroyed Jerusalem in 586 BC, carrying many Judeans into exile. Yet Babylon's dominance as a world power did not last much longer after that. With little struggle, Cyrus of Persia conquered Babylon by 539 BC.

Cyrus had come to power initially under the authority of the more powerful Median Empire. The Medes controlled a vast amount of territory north and east of the Babylonian Empire. Within roughly a decade, however, Cyrus conquered the Medes, assumed their territory, and declared himself king of Persia (modern Iran). His empire is thus referred to as either the Persian Empire or the Medo-Persian Empire.

The Persians ruled over the Judeans in a much more benevolent manner than the Babylonians had. The Persians sponsored the Jews' return to Jerusalem of 538 BC, allowing the Jewish people to rule themselves by their own laws. There were, of course, strings attached. Should the Jews rebel or withhold tribute, the Persians would beat them into submission.

This arrangement lasted until the 330s BC. At that time, Alexander the Great of Greece subdued the Persians and took control of Palestine. Alexander died in 323 BC, and his kingdom was divided among his generals. These Greek rulers continued Persia's more benevolent foreign policy for the most part. This lasted until about the middle of the second century BC, when the tide changed for the worse for God's people (see the non-biblical book of 1 Maccabees). Daniel's vision in today's lesson provides an important glimpse into some terrifying periods and God's decisive response.

HOW TO SAY IT

Antiochus Epiphanes	An-*tie*-oh-kus Ih-*piff*-a-neez.
apocalypse	uh-*pock*-uh-lips.
apocalyptic	uh-*pock*-uh-***lip***-tik.
Belshazzar	Bel-*shazz*-er.
Lysimachus	Lie-*sih*-meh-kus.
Maccabees	*Mack*-uh-bees.
Macedon	*Mah*-suh-dun.
Medes	Meeds.
Ptolemy	*Tahl*-uh-me.
Seleucus	Suh-*loo*-kuss.
Ulai	*You*-lye or *You*-luh-eye.

I. Meeting the Interpreter

(Daniel 8:1, 15-19)

A. Second Vision Is Received (v. 1)

1. In the third year of the reign of king Belshazzar a vision appeared unto me, even unto me Daniel, after that which appeared unto me at the first.

The third year of the reign of king Belshazzar of Babylon computes to 550 BC, about 36 years after the fall of Jerusalem. As noted in Lesson 1, Belshazzar was a wicked ruler who made sport of the sacred vessels that were confiscated from the Jerusalem temple (Daniel 5). It is thus fitting that this particular vision, which concerns a future arrogant king who also makes sport of the Jewish faith (see Daniel 8:23-25, below), takes place during the reign of Belshazzar.

The substance of Daniel's vision is presented in Daniel 8:3-14, although that section is not included in today's text. As we focus on the interpretation of the vision, we will be referring to verses 3-14 as necessary to help us understand the interpretation. The vision of four beasts in Daniel 7 (last week's lesson) is likely the one described here as *that which appeared unto me at the first.*

B. Gabriel Is Commissioned (vv. 15, 16)

15. And it came to pass, when I, even I Daniel, had seen the vision, and sought for the meaning, then, behold, there stood before me as the appearance of a man.

Daniel tries to understand what he has seen thus far; the vision is not yet ended. Explanation begins to come with *the appearance of a man.* This figure should not be confused with the one who looks "like the Son of man" in Daniel 7:13. The word used here for *man* in the original language is different. It is a technical term meaning "mighty one" (example: Isaiah 42:13), and it is nearly identical to the name of the vision's interpreter (next verse).

16. And I heard a man's voice between the banks of Ulai, which called, and said, Gabriel, make this man to understand the vision.

Daniel is still near the Ulai River, the place where he saw himself at the beginning of his vision (Daniel 8:2). In this part of the vision, Daniel hears an unidentified voice calling to the one who looks like a man in verse 15. This man is named Gabriel, which means "mighty one of God" in the original language. Gabriel is appointed to help Daniel *understand the vision.* Gabriel will make another appearance about 28 years later, in Daniel 9:21 (compare Luke 1:19, 26).

C. Daniel Is Resuscitated (vv. 17, 18)

17. So he came near where I stood: and when he came, I was afraid, and fell upon my face: but he said unto me, Understand, O son of man: for at the time of the end shall be the vision.

Daniel is terrified as Gabriel approaches. Reverence and fear are common reactions throughout the Scriptures when humans encounter angelic beings (examples: Numbers 22:31; Joshua 5:14; Luke 1:12; Acts 10:3, 4; Revelation 19:10).

Daniel must understand that the vision concerns not the time of his own day in the mid–sixth century BC, but *the time at the end.* The phrase *the end* can be interpreted in more than one way, depending on context.

Sometimes *the end* means "the end of history as we know it," which comes about when Jesus returns. In other instances, *the end* refers to the end of a specific time period in history (example: Ezekiel 7:1-7). In still other cases, it seems to be both, as if the events of the somewhat near future are only the beginning of a long string of events that find their fulfillment in the final judgment and reign of Christ. We will dig into this further as the interpretation of the vision unfolds.

What Do You Think?

What circumstances, if any, should cause us to react in reverence as Daniel did? Why?

Talking Points for Your Discussion

- Deuteronomy 9:18, 25
- 1 Chronicles 29:20
- Ecclesiastes 3:7b
- Habakkuk 2:20
- Revelation 5:8, 14; 7:11; 19:4

18. Now as he was speaking with me, I was in a deep sleep on my face toward the ground: but he touched me, and set me upright.

The appearance of Gabriel has so startled Daniel that he has fainted or is otherwise knocked out cold! But Daniel needs to be prepared to hear the message, so Gabriel revives him and sets him on his feet. Though God's messengers are frightening to behold, humans can nonetheless handle being in their presence. Angels are to be respected as God's messengers, but they are not to be worshipped (see Revelation 19:9, 10 and 22:8, 9).

D. Interpretation Is Introduced (v. 19)

19. And he said, Behold, I will make thee know what shall be in the last end of the indignation: for at the time appointed the end shall be.

When Gabriel first speaks to Daniel in verse 17, he tells him that the vision pertains to "the end." Gabriel's decision to repeat that here may indicate that Daniel did not hear him the first time, having lost consciousness.

Regardless, Gabriel adds at this point that the end being discussed is *appointed,* presumably by God. This means that as disturbing as the events may be, God remains in control. He knows what is going to happen, and He will somehow bring events in line with His plans. This does not mean that God will cause the events to happen or is pleased by them. His power is demonstrated in the fact that He takes disordered human decisions and orders them for His own saving purposes.

Some Things Can't Be Rushed

For every expectant mother who patiently contemplates the new life growing inside her, there are a dozen others who are ready for their baby to be born now! Folk advice abounds on how to hurry labor. My wife's aunt had her husband drive over bouncy country roads in an attempt to initiate labor, to no effect. A wise grandmother gave probably the best advice: "That baby will come when she wants to come."

We easily imagine Daniel's mixed emotions at the troubling visions and interpretations. Yes, his people would be delivered, but their salvation would involve further suffering first. Like receiving news of a needed surgery, this message must have brought a mixture of dread and anticipation. Gabriel's words brought reassurance that everything was going according to plan; Daniel had only to wait.

Finishing school, paying off debt, recuperating from illness—such things can make us feel like something is holding us back from achieving our goals. Modern technology allows us to speed many things up, but some things simply can't be rushed. Strained relationships can take a long time to heal. Non-Christian friends aren't always receptive to our witness. God will work all our experiences together for good (Romans 8:28), but we dare not try to rush His timing. —A. W.

What Do You Think?

When was a time you resisted (or failed to resist) the temptation to try to rush God's timing? How did things turn out?

Talking Points for Your Discussion

- In making a vocational choice
- In starting a church building program
- In making a personal commitment
- Numbers 14:40-45
- Other

II. Receiving the Interpretation
(Daniel 8:20-26)

A. Ram Is Identified (v. 20)

20. The ram which thou sawest having two horns are the kings of Media and Persia.

The first thing Daniel saw in his vision, back in verse 3, was a ram standing beside the Ulai River. One of its two horns is "higher" than the other. The ram moves relentlessly in triumph "westward, and northward, and southward" (v. 4). These details align perfectly with Gabriel's statement that the ram represents *Media and Persia.* The facts of history affirm that the Medo-Persian kingdom expands in these three directions.

The ram is depicted fittingly in Daniel 8:3 as a single animal with two horns of unequal length since Media and Persia are two kingdoms that collapse into one, with the Cyrus of Persia becoming prominent (see the Lesson Background). The disproportionate horn length may be parallel to the image of the bear in the previous vision that was raised up on one side (Daniel 7:5).

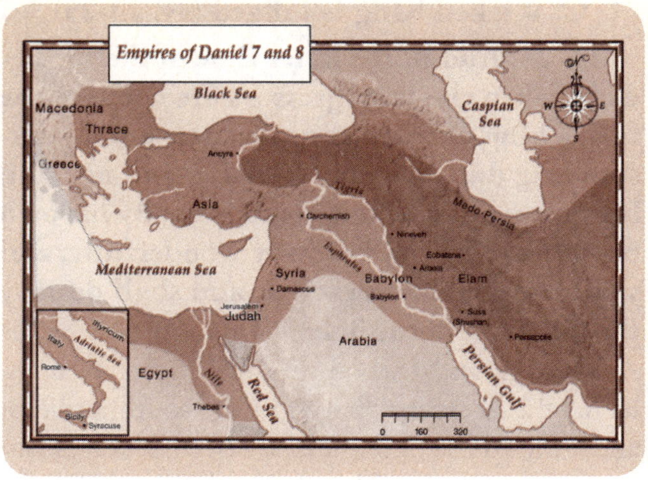

Visual for Lessons 1 & 3. *Help your learners keep a geographical perspective by referring to this map frequently as you study the three lessons of Unit 1.*

B. Goat Is Identified (vv. 21, 22)

21. And the rough goat is the king of Grecia: and the great horn that is between his eyes is the first king.

The animal of Daniel 8:5-7 is a one-horned goat that charges from the west, tramples the ram, and shatters the ram's two horns. Gabriel now identifies this animal as *the king of Grecia* (Greece). The record of history informs us that *the great horn . . . the first king* is Alexander the Great, who will be born about 194 years after this vision. After coming to power, Alexander moves quickly from west to east to take control of the Medo-Persian Empire.

22. Now that being broken, whereas four stood up for it, four kingdoms shall stand up out of the nation, but not in his power.

According to Daniel 8:8, the great horn is broken as it becomes strong, being replaced with four horns pointing "toward the four winds of heaven." Gabriel clarifies here that these horns are four kingdoms that lack Alexander's power.

This is exactly what ends up happening historically. Alexander dies at age 33 in 323 BC, and His kingdom eventually is divided among four of his generals: Cassander rules over Macedon and Greece (west); Lysimachus rules Thrace and Asia Minor (north); Seleucus rules Syria and Babylon (east); and Ptolemy rules Egypt (south). Since each of these kingdoms receives only a portion of Alexander's empire, none of them matches *his power.*

C. Wicked King Is Judged (vv. 23-25)

23, 24. And in the latter time of their kingdom, when the transgressors are come to the full, a king of fierce countenance, and understanding dark sentences, shall stand up. And his power shall be mighty, but not by his own power: and he shall destroy wonderfully, and shall prosper, and practise, and shall destroy the mighty and the holy people.

These verses focus on the "little horn" of Daniel 8:9-12. It wreaks havoc in the south and east and "toward the pleasant land" (v. 9). It wages war against "the host of heaven," "the prince of the host," and even "the place of his sanctuary" (vv. 10, 11). No one seems able to stop this rampaging king.

Gabriel clarifies here that this king comes later than the others and that he stands out in ferocity and darkness. In particular, this king seeks to destroy *the holy people.* This is Gabriel's way of identifying "the pleasant land" of verse 9. That land is Judah. The Greek king most known for attacking God's people in their homeland is Antiochus IV, also known as Antiochus Epiphanes. He rules from 175 to 164 BC.

It is not clear what it means that this king's prosperity is not *by his own power.* The book of Daniel makes no reference to satanic influence. If the reference is to God, the point is that Antiochus can have power over God's people only as God allows it. Any power Antiochus is to have will be on loan from God. This does not mean that God is the cause of this king's wicked deeds. But it *does* mean that God can easily take that man's power away.

What Do You Think?

What are some ways that Christians should respond and not respond to an oppressive government?

Talking Points for Your Discussion

- Matthew 5:39
- Mark 12:17
- Luke 2:1-4
- Acts 4:19; 5:29; 16:35-37; 22:25
- Romans 13:1-7
- Ephesians 6:12
- 1 Peter 2:17

25. And through his policy also he shall cause craft to prosper in his hand; and he shall magnify himself in his heart, and by peace shall destroy many: he shall also stand up against the Prince of princes; but he shall be broken without hand.

Wickedness thrives during the reign of Antiochus. Jews with money and a willingness to abandon faith can rise to prominence within his corrupt regime. Jews who resist his policies are persecuted from 170 to 164 BC. Antiochus ends up being so arrogant that he rises up against God himself by defiling the Jerusalem temple in 167 BC. Jews are killed for reading Scriptures, honoring the Sabbath, abstaining from unclean food, etc. (This is described in the nonbiblical 1 Maccabees 1:54-61.)

This period proves to be one of the most distressing eras in Jewish history. Yet God is still in control. The verse before us ends with a clear and simple statement that Antiochus *shall be broken,* although not by human agency *(without hand).* God is the one who brings him to justice. When God decides that the time is right, He will destroy Antiochus as easily as he does the ferocious beast in Daniel 7:11. This remarkable prophecy is given over 380 years before it comes to pass!

What Do You Think?

How do we know when we should "let God handle it" and not try to "assist" Him?

Talking Points for Your Discussion

- Deuteronomy 32:35 (Hebrews 10:30)
- Isaiah 6:8-10 (Acts 28:26)
- Ezekiel 22:30
- Zechariah 4:6b
- Matthew 28:19, 20

D. Vision Is Sealed (v. 26)

26a. And the vision of the evening and the morning which was told is true.

The last thing Daniel heard before Gabriel began revealing his interpretation in Daniel 8:17 was an angelic voice stating that the sanctuary is to be restored "unto two thousand and three hundred days" (v. 14). Gabriel now stresses that this will indeed happen. God will not allow His holy place to be violated indefinitely.

This prophecy is fulfilled in 164 BC, three years after the temple's defilement; that's when the temple is rededicated. Three years adds up to roughly 1,150 days or a combination of 2,300 evenings and mornings (see 1 Maccabees 4:36-58).

26b. Wherefore shut thou up the vision; for it shall be for many days.

What is fascinating about this passage is what Daniel is *not* called to do: he is not charged to do anything to keep these terrible events from happening. Instead, he is told to seal up the vision and wait for it to unfold.

The purpose of this advance notice is not to keep certain things from happening, but to help the reader develop a "God's-eye view" of these events when they do happen. Those faithful to God must trust that God is in control; in the midst of persecution, God's people are to bear witness to their trust in that fact.

Good Secrets

We are keeping a secret from our daughter. In a few months, my wife is taking her on her first overseas trip to visit friends on the mission field. At just 9 years old, she will be deeply affected by this experience, perhaps even becoming inspired to be a missionary herself one day.

But there is no way we are going to tell her about the trip now! If we did, she would be distracted from her schoolwork, have tension with her younger siblings, and perhaps even dread the thought of the trip rather than look forward to it. Even though what we plan is a good thing, her not knowing is, in our judgment, better for her right now than knowing.

God told Daniel about some future events, but not all the precise details regarding Israel's future rescue. Likewise, God does not lay out detailed road maps of everything that He has in store for us. Think about it: if as a child you had been given to know everything that would happen to you by now, would you have been able to understand it or bear it? May we praise the all-wise God who tells us just what we need to know when we need to know it! See 1 Corinthians 2:9. —A. W.

What Do You Think?

How do you resist the danger of becoming overly fascinated with the intricacies of prophecy?

Talking Points for Your Discussion

- Ways to achieve balance in Bible study
- Counsel from spiritually mature Christians
- Prayer
- Other

Conclusion

A. Apocalypse Now!

If Daniel 8 is an indication of how biblical apocalypses function, then there are a few lessons that we learn about how to read them. We learn about the nature of symbolic language. We learn that God does not give us glimpses into the future so we can use that knowledge to take control of how things turn out. We learn that sometimes God gives us only enough knowledge of the future to embolden us to remain radically faithful in the present.

Yet not all apocalyptic texts are the same. Daniel 8 is different in many ways from Daniel 7 and Daniel 10–12. The book of Daniel as a whole is different from the book of Revelation, which in Greek is called *Apocalypse.* Yet these differences are not so great that a proper reading of Daniel cannot prepare us for a proper reading of Revelation. Though some of the events foretold in Revelation pertain to the end of time when Jesus brings His kingdom in its fullness, much of that book also pertains to events of the first-century church. In all this, one thing remains clear: God is in control. May we approach God's Word with that fact in mind. Our side wins.

B. Prayer

Lord God, we confess that You are Lord over world history. Deliver us from the temptation to try seizing control. Give us eyes to see the bigger picture and to embrace a future that ultimately is in Your benevolent arms. In Jesus' name, amen.

C. Thought to Remember

God is faithful and able to deliver His people.

Involvement Learning

Some of the activities below are also found in the helpful student book, Adult Bible Class.
Don't forget to download the free reproducible page from www.standardlesson.com to enhance your lesson!

Into the Lesson

Early in the week, ask one of your learners to prepare a mini-lecture of the Lesson Background. Display or project a map of the world powers being described during the presentation. If you don't have such a map, create and distribute handouts of one (easy to find on the Internet).

Option: Before class, place in chairs copies of the "Visions and Interpretations" activity from the reproducible page, which you can download. Learners can begin working on this as they arrive (before the mini-lecture above). After discussing results, say, "God does not always provide interpretations of symbolic language, but we sure do appreciate it when He does! Today's study takes us to one such instance. But first we need some background." Then introduce the mini-lecture above.

Into the Word

Have learners take turns reading aloud the verses of today's printed text, Daniel 8:1, 15-26. *Alternative:* Learners can read the entirety of Daniel 8, but this will be a lengthy reading.

Option 1: Distribute copies of the "Proofreading Prophecy" activity from the reproducible page, which you can download. Say, "This will be a closed-Bible quiz. You get one point for circling each wrong item, and one point for writing the correct answer to replace the wrong item; thus there are 26 points possible. As soon as you are finished, open your Bible and score the quiz yourself." (*Alternative:* You can have learners work as open-Bible study pairs.) Identify the two or three most missed errors for special attention.

Option 2: Write the following answers on the board in a scattered manner: *Alexander the Great, Antiochus Epiphanes, Belshazzar, Daniel, Gabriel.* Then distribute the following short notes to volunteers to be read aloud in a "Who Am I?" activity. Point to the names on the board as you say, "These individuals are part of today's text. See if you can match names with descriptions." Distribute eight slips of paper to eight learners, one each. The slips will have the following statements, one per slip. Direct readers to read the clue statements but not the answer.

1. I was a conquering king. Daniel's vision pictured me as a mighty, shaggy goat from the west. *(Alexander the Great; see Daniel 8:21)* 2. I spoke on behalf of God to Daniel, and I also spoke for God to two people in Luke 1. *(Gabriel; see Daniel 8:15, 16; Luke 1:19, 26)* 3. I was a wicked king who inherited a small portion of Alexander's empire. I desecrated the Jews' holy place. *(Antiochus Epiphanes; see the lesson notes on Daniel 8:23-25)* 4. As king, I saw "the handwriting on the wall." This happened as I was desecrating the holy vessels of the Jerusalem temple. *(Belshazzar; see Daniel 5:1-5; 8:1)* 5. Through Gabriel I received the meaning of my vision as a hope for my people Israel. *(Daniel)*

Into Life

Say, "God's sovereignty is an important concept in today's study." Discuss dictionary definitions of the words *sovereign* and *sovereignty* with your class. Then give each learner a copy of this acrostic:

S—supreme, Savior
O—overcomer, omnipotent, omniscient
V—victorious, vision-giving
E—eternal, excellent, enabler
R—righteous, ruler, revealer
E—everlasting, elevated (on a throne)
I—invincible, invisible, indivisible (yet triune)
G—gracious, governing
N—not limited, not defeated

Say, "In your devotional times this week, see how many of these concepts you can introduce into your prayers as you praise God for His sovereignty over history." Use some of the above concepts in closing your class with prayer. Distribute copies of the "Standing Against the Prince of Princes" from the reproducible page as a take-home activity.

The Lord's Supper

Devotional Reading: 1 Corinthians 10:14-22
Background Scripture: Luke 22:1-38

Luke 22:14-30

14 And when the hour was come, he sat down, and the twelve apostles with him.

15 And he said unto them, With desire I have desired to eat this passover with you before I suffer:

16 For I say unto you, I will not any more eat thereof, until it be fulfilled in the kingdom of God.

17 And he took the cup, and gave thanks, and said, Take this, and divide it among yourselves:

18 For I say unto you, I will not drink of the fruit of the vine, until the kingdom of God shall come.

19 And he took bread, and gave thanks, and brake it, and gave unto them, saying, This is my body which is given for you: this do in remembrance of me.

20 Likewise also the cup after supper, saying, This cup is the new testament in my blood, which is shed for you.

21 But, behold, the hand of him that betrayeth me is with me on the table.

22 And truly the Son of man goeth, as it was determined: but woe unto that man by whom he is betrayed!

23 And they began to enquire among themselves, which of them it was that should do this thing.

24 And there was also a strife among them, which of them should be accounted the greatest.

25 And he said unto them, The kings of the Gentiles exercise lordship over them; and they that exercise authority upon them are called benefactors.

26 But ye shall not be so: but he that is greatest among you, let him be as the younger; and he that is chief, as he that doth serve.

27 For whether is greater, he that sitteth at meat, or he that serveth? is not he that sitteth at meat? but I am among you as he that serveth.

28 Ye are they which have continued with me in my temptations.

29 And I appoint unto you a kingdom, as my Father hath appointed unto me;

30 That ye may eat and drink at my table in my kingdom, and sit on thrones judging the twelve tribes of Israel.

Key Verse

He that is greatest among you, let him be as the younger; and he that is chief, as he that doth serve.

—Luke 22:26b

Photo: Dynamic Graphics / Liquidlibrary / Thinkstock

Undying Hope

Unit 2: Resurrection Hope

Lessons 4–9

Lesson Aims

After participating in this lesson, each student will be able to:

1. Retell the events of the instituting of the Lord's Supper.

2. Note the irony of the disciples' dispute about who was the greatest as juxtaposed against Jesus' words about His impending sacrifice.

3. Confess that he or she sometimes focuses on self even in the midst of worship events that focus on Christ.

Lesson Outline

Introduction
- A. Last Supper, Lord's Supper
- B. Lesson Background

I. Somber Celebration (Luke 22:14-20)
- A. Last Passover (vv. 14-16)
- B. Last Cup (vv. 17, 18)
- C. Last Loaf (v. 19)
- D. New Covenant (v. 20)

II. Sobering Prediction (Luke 22:21-30)
- A. Hand of Betrayal (vv. 21, 22)
  - *Famous (or Infamous) Traitors*
- B. Head of Boasting (vv. 23, 24)
  - *"Getting It"—or Not!*
- C. Heart of Service (vv. 25-27)
- D. Honor of Faithfulness (vv. 28-30)

Conclusion
- A. Remembering
- B. Prayer
- C. Thought to Remember

Introduction

A. Last Supper, Lord's Supper

Christians have shared in the Lord's Supper millions of times in the last 2,000 years. These celebrations trace their origin to a single meal shared by Jesus and His disciples in an upstairs room in Jerusalem. That was a bittersweet time for Jesus: He had looked forward to this fellowship meal, yet He knew that He would be betrayed that night by one of His friends. He knew that that betrayal would set in motion a series of events leading to His crucifixion.

At that historic meal, Jesus asked His disciples to remember Him whenever they reenacted the meal in the future. This week's lesson studies Luke's account of this meal so that we might better understand and remember what our Savior faced on that night.

B. Lesson Background

Each of the four Gospels has an account of the last supper, with varying details. For example, John records the meal, but makes no mention of the institution of the Lord's Supper by Jesus. Luke is unique is telling of more than one cup used by Jesus. These distinctives are not in conflict, and each adds to the rich picture of the last supper.

Luke 22:7, which precedes today's lesson text, describes the occasion of the last supper as "the day of unleavened bread, when the passover [lamb] must be killed." This would have been Friday, before the Sabbath/Saturday of that week. We must remember, however, that most Jews reckoned a new day as beginning at sundown, so their Friday would have begun at sundown on Thursday by our system. Sundown would have been at about 6 PM, so this Passover celebration by Jesus and His disciples probably took place within the time frame of 7–10 PM on Thursday night by modern reckoning.

I. Somber Celebration

(Luke 22:14-20)

A. Last Passover (vv. 14-16)

14. And when the hour was come, he sat down, and the twelve apostles with him.

Mention of *the hour* indicates the time for the meal after all the preparations are finished. These preparations likely include the provision of a low table with pillowed couches around it. If such a configuration is correct, then *sat down* means that the participants are reclining on their sides (compare Matthew 26:20).

15. And he said unto them, With desire I have desired to eat this passover with you before I suffer.

Jesus' opening comments introduce both a uniqueness and a sense of finality to this meal. He reveals (again) that He anticipates a disturbing thing that is coming: His suffering. This is the word sometimes translated as "passion" (see Acts 1:3); it refers to the humiliation and pain that Jesus endures in His trials, flogging, and being nailed to a wooden cross to die.

The writers of the Gospels present Jesus as being aware of this inevitable passion-time. These writers also depict the disciples as being generally oblivious in this regard. It is doubtful that any of those 12 imagine that the lifeless body of Jesus will be lying in a tomb less than 24 hours after this meal concludes.

16. For I say unto you, I will not any more eat thereof, until it be fulfilled in the kingdom of God.

At the same time, Jesus introduces a note of hopeful anticipation. He reveals that He will eat again, but only under very different circumstances. His future eating will be in connection with the fulfillment of *the kingdom of God.* This will be feasting on the other side of death, celebration in a new reality. We are reminded of Jesus' picture of a future messianic banquet (see Luke 14:15-24; 22:29, 30), a table where people from all nations will be welcome (13:29).

B. Last Cup (vv. 17, 18)

17. And he took the cup, and gave thanks, and said, Take this, and divide it among yourselves.

Luke mentions two instances in which Jesus and the disciples share a cup at this meal: here and in verse 20 (below). Since this is a Passover feast (called *seder* by modern Jews), there are several traditional parts to the meal. We do not know exactly how Jesus and His disciples organize these traditions, but celebration of a modern seder involves drinking from four cups during the meal. Some identify the cup in this verse with the seder's third cup, called "the cup of blessing."

The Greek word behind *gave thanks* is the origin of the word *Eucharist.* This designation is used in some Christian traditions for the Lord's Supper.

18. For I say unto you, I will not drink of the fruit of the vine, until the kingdom of God shall come.

As in verse 16, Jesus emphasizes the finality of this occasion. There will be no more festive meals for Him *until the kingdom of God shall come.*

There is debate over what constitutes the establishment *(shall come)* of God's kingdom. Luke 24:41-43 records that Jesus does indeed eat with His disciples after His resurrection. But there is no indication that that meal involves *the fruit of the vine,* and it certainly is not a Passover celebration. We should understand that the language of the verse before us indicates a transition: Jesus and His followers are moving from one era into another. In the new era, Jesus' disciples (Christians) will share the cup with Jesus each time they reenact this last supper as the Lord's Supper.

What Do You Think?

How can we keep the Lord's Supper from becoming a source of division rather than unity?

Talking Points for Your Discussion

- Differences in doctrinal interpretation
- Undue focus on accessories
- Entrenched traditions
- Other

There is also debate over what is meant by *fruit of the vine.* If taken literally, this refers to grapes. But you do not drink grapes, so we can assume that Jesus is referring to the juice of grapes. The debate concerns whether or not this juice is fermented—whether it is wine or fresh grape juice.

Many scholars conclude that it is unlikely that first-century Jews would use fresh grape juice at a Passover meal, so they think that it is wine. Others stress the point that the gospel texts say *fruit of the vine* specifically (Matthew 26:29; Mark 14:25), not *wine* as in, for example, Acts 2:13. At any rate, the importance in using this beverage is not its alcohol content, but its color. It is a deep red with a hint of blue—a purplish-red color we call *crimson.* This is very close to the color of blood, making this cup filled with the fruit of the vine a meaningful symbol for use in the Lord's Supper (see Luke 22:20, below).

C. Last Loaf (v. 19)

19. And he took bread, and gave thanks, and brake it, and gave unto them, saying, This is my body which is given for you: this do in remembrance of me.

Passover traditions dictate that bread used at this feast be baked without leaven (yeast). This is in accordance with the first Passover meal, celebrated on the eve of the Israelites' departure from Egypt. On that occasion, the people needed to bake their bread quickly, not having time for dough to rise. Thus it was unleavened (Exodus 12, especially v. 39).

After giving thanks again (see also Luke 24:30), Jesus makes two enduring comments. The first one is the statement *this is my body.* Some Christian traditions take this to mean that the bread used in Communion services today is somehow transformed into the physical body of Christ. However, this is not what Jesus intends for us to understand. The rich symbolism of the bread lies in breaking the loaf (as Christ's body is damaged on the cross), in giving the loaf (as Christ gives His life willingly as a sacrifice for our sins), and in the sharing of the loaf among all participants (as Christians share a common faith in Christ).

The other enduring comment is the command *this do in remembrance of me.* This indicates two things. First, there is a coming time when the disciples of Jesus will celebrate this meal without His being physically present—after all, you don't have to "remember" someone who is right there with you physically. Jesus is to be remembered for all He did and said, and most of all for the salvation His death provides (see Hebrews 10:10).

Second, Jesus' command indicates that the disciples are to reenact His symbolic actions in the future. As they do, the last supper becomes the Lord's Supper in the church (compare 1 Corinthians 11:20-26).

What Do You Think?

Besides *this do in remembrance of me,* what would be some good inscriptions for Communion tables?

Talking Points for Your Discussion

- Matthew 26:26, 27
- Mark 14:24
- Luke 22:17
- Acts 2:42
- 1 Corinthians 11:26
- Other

D. New Covenant (v. 20)

20. Likewise also the cup after supper, saying, This cup is the new testament in my blood, which is shed for you.

The word *likewise* indicates that this particular cup is also blessed with a thanksgiving and shared among the disciples. As already mentioned, a traditional Passover meal can involve several cups, each symbolizing something different. With this final cup of the evening, Jesus ties the contents of the cup to His death. He does so by comparing the cup with His blood, which is soon to be shed in His upcoming torture and crucifixion.

The fact that this cup signifies *the new testament* indicates a new agreement between God and humanity. This is the new covenant promised in Jeremiah 31:31-34, a covenant of forgiveness (compare Exodus 24:8). The old regime of law is passing, and a new era of grace is beginning. Whenever we drink the cup in our celebrations of the Lord's Supper, we should remember what a great blessing it is to live under this covenant.

II. Sobering Prediction

(Luke 22:21-30)

A. Hand of Betrayal (vv. 21, 22)

21, 22. But, behold, the hand of him that betrayeth me is with me on the table. And truly the Son of man goeth, as it was determined: but woe unto that man by whom he is betrayed!

The reality of dark deeds yet to come again creeps into the meal. We easily imagine that Jesus' tone of voice changes dramatically as He reveals that there is a traitor within the group. While there have been warnings about this before (see John 6:70, 71), this is the most blatant declaration thus far. Jesus demonstrates His divine knowledge of the plot against Him (compare Luke 22:1-6).

Jesus also reveals that His own future *was determined,* meaning that it has been part of God's plan for human salvation all along. Judas Iscariot's act of betrayal accomplishes God's purpose, but Judas's decision to turn traitor is his own choice, foreseen by God (Acts 1:16-20); Judas will be held responsible for his treachery (1:25).

Judas's actions remain one of the great mysteries of human history. How could one who was on such close terms with the Savior of the world betray his friend and teacher? We do not understand this fully, but Luke records that Judas is motivated by the presence of Satan in his heart (Luke 22:3) and the lure of money (22:5).

What Do You Think?

What are some ways people betray Jesus today? How do you protect yourself from doing so?

Talking Points for Your Discussion

- In thought life
- In the workplace
- In entertainment choices
- "Don't assume you are the good soil [of Luke 8:15]" (Francis Chan, *Crazy Love*).
- Other

Famous (or Infamous) Traitors

Benedict Arnold had a distinguished career during America's Revolutionary War. Some of his military actions on land and water were simply brilliant. But Arnold was not nearly as good at "playing politics," and he was passed over for promotion as a result. In anger, he negotiated with the British and planned to turn over to them the American fort at West Point.

The unsuccessful plot resulted in Arnold's name becoming virtually synonymous with the word *traitor;* it is a label that overshadows all of Arnold's military successes. When someone is referred to as "a Benedict Arnold," we instinctively know that the reference is not to that man's military brilliance!

The same is true of Judas Iscariot. As an apostle, he took part in the magnificent physical and spiritual victories described in Luke 9:1-6. But to call someone "a Judas" today is not to affirm that person's devotion to the work of the Lord—quite the opposite! The church has had her traitors and defectors throughout the centuries. We do well to remember that "No man, having put his hand to the plough, and looking back, is fit for the kingdom of God" (Luke 9:62). —C. R. B.

B. Head of Boasting (vv. 23, 24)

23, 24. And they began to enquire among themselves, which of them it was that should do this thing. And there was also a strife among them, which of them should be accounted the greatest.

In the chaotic discussion that follows, we can imagine each disciple trying to outdo his companions by pledging higher and higher levels of loyalty to Jesus. At some point, this discussion seems to degenerate, making a transition from claims of having the greatest love for the Master to claims of being the greatest (compare Luke 9:46).

This discussion seems nearly insane from our perspective. Yet Jesus uses this confusion to give one of His last teaching lessons before the crucifixion.

What Do You Think?

Is there any place for a competitive spirit within the church? Why, or why not?

Talking Points for Your Discussion

- 1 Corinthians 11:19
- Philippians 2:3
- Hebrews 10:24
- Other?

"Getting It"—or Not!

"You just don't get it!" is a common expression of frustration when people are disagreeing about something. It is a way of characterizing someone as uncaring or clueless. A wife may use this expression when her husband fails to perceive the level of importance she places on his attendance at a dinner with her family. In turn, he may use this expression when she doesn't grasp the importance of his playing golf for the second time in a week as part of the process of sealing a business deal.

We can imagine Jesus thinking *You just don't get it* during the last supper. He was trying to prepare His disciples for what He would be facing later that evening and the following morning. There He was about to confront the greatest crisis of His life, and His disciples were arguing over who would be greatest! They "didn't get it."

"Not getting it" can result from *tunnel vision,* an extreme narrowness of viewpoint. Jesus had to confront tunnel vision throughout His earthly ministry. May we heed both the problem and Jesus' responses to it. —C. R. B.

C. Heart of Service (vv. 25-27)

25. And he said unto them, The kings of the Gentiles exercise lordship over them; and they that exercise authority upon them are called benefactors.

Rather than condemning the disciples for vying for position, Jesus uses an example that grabs their attention: that of earthly rulers. This includes the Romans, the hated occupiers of the Jewish homeland. Jesus' point is that the kings and other rulers exercise their power over people in a self-serving manner while thinking of themselves as benefactors in the process. Jesus' implication is that these Gentile rulers primarily benefit themselves. This underlying truth is well-known to Jesus' disciples.

26. But ye shall not be so: but he that is greatest among you, let him be as the younger; and he that is chief, as he that doth serve.

HOW TO SAY IT

Eucharist	*You*-kuh-rust.
Gethsemane	Geth-*sem*-uh-nee (G as in *get*).
Judas Iscariot	*Joo*-dus Iss-*care*-ee-ut.
messianic	mess-ee-*an*-ick.
seder	*say*-der.

Having established the pattern of self-serving rulers, Jesus gives two other examples of social priority to make his point. Younger men of the first century are considered social inferiors to their elders. Slaves or servants are always in a lesser position than their masters. Jesus turns this leadership model inside out by proclaiming the greatest one is not the person ordering others around, but the one who serves others.

27. For whether is greater, he that sitteth at meat, or he that serveth? is not he that sitteth at meat? but I am among you as he that serveth.

Jesus goes on to use the example of a banquet, asking if the one who is being served *(he that sitteth at meat)* is greater than the one who serves. This is the image of the rich man who presides over a lavish feast versus the servant who brings the food and clears the dishes. The immediate assumption of the rich man being the greater is thrown out when Jesus places himself in the role of the servant. Greatness in God's kingdom is found in serving others rather than self.

What Do You Think?

When was a time you were surprised to be blessed as you served someone else?

Talking Points for Your Discussion

- In a benevolence setting
- In a teaching setting
- In a counseling setting
- Other

D. Honor of Faithfulness (vv. 28-30)

28. Ye are they which have continued with me in my temptations.

Jesus turns from His corrective rebuke to commend His disciples for staying true to Him during His temptations. By this Jesus refers to the times when He and His disciples were in physical danger from Jesus' opponents (compare John 11:8, 16). He may also be referring to the satanic attacks that were present throughout His ministry.

Sadly, however, the disciples will fall asleep during Jesus' great trial of agony in the Garden of Gethsemane (Luke 22:39-46). This disappointing performance by the disciples will be minor compared with what follows, however. When a mob led by one of the disciples comes to arrest Jesus, the disciples will abandon Jesus in the darkness and confusion.

29, 30. And I appoint unto you a kingdom, as my Father hath appointed unto me; that ye may eat and drink at my table in my kingdom, and sit on thrones judging the twelve tribes of Israel.

Finally, Jesus points the disciples to a wondrous future time when there will be another great fellowship meal. This will be in Jesus' kingdom. It is a marvelous image: a lavish table of food and drink, with the disciples reunited with Jesus. They will no longer be reclining on cushions since the table will be crowded with thrones for Jesus and the disciples. The disciples will have judging authority over the people of God, represented as *the twelve tribes of Israel.* But Jesus is the master king at this table, for it is His table. He is the King of kings, as appointed by God.

Conclusion

A. Remembering

Collective memory is important. It has been said that the one who controls the memories of a community controls its future. Some cultures value elderly people because they are the ones whose memory stretches back the furthest. As important as the issue of remembering is, however, another important issue is that of forgetting.

Sometimes we wish we had more control over our forgetting, for there are things we would like to forget but cannot. But certain things should be—must be—remembered. A memory that is neglected and unused will fade over the years. Memory works best when it is "jogged." How do we jog our memories about the most important things in life, things that must not be lost? Families may do this by taking out photo albums of past events, remembering loved ones who are gone but not forgotten. The church has a superb way of remembering the essential truths of the Christian faith in its celebration of the Lord's Supper.

Although there may be many variations in its practice, the Lord's Supper should always serve to

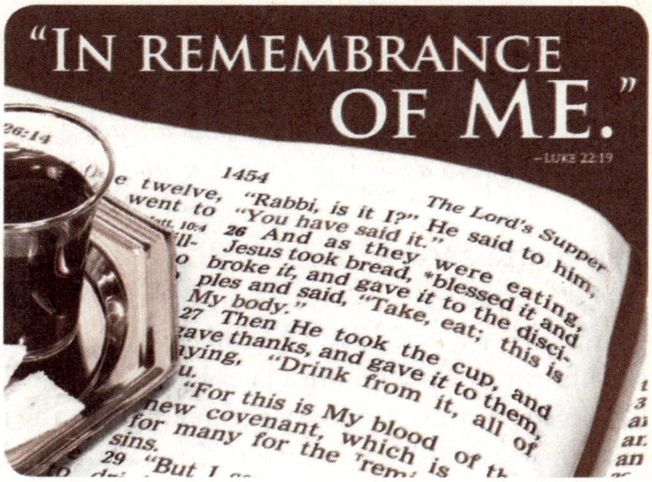

Visual for Lesson 4. *As you study verse 19, point to this visual and ask, "How can we better prepare ourselves for observing the Lord's Supper?"*

help us remember. The broken bread we use helps us remember the body of Christ, broken in the death on that lonely cross outside of Jerusalem. The cup should help us remember that our salvation was made possible through the blood of Christ, given freely as an acceptable sacrifice for our sins.

A paradox of the Lord's Supper is that while it symbolizes bloody brokenness, it is also a great unifying factor for the church. We remember Christ's body broken for us, but we should also look for the unbroken body, the church, which is the body of Christ on earth. We should share around the Lord's table in fellowship, not isolation. This is why it is called *Communion,* for we have communing fellowship with other Christians and with the Lord.

The next time you participate in your church's celebration of the Lord's Supper, take time to remember these things: blood as a price for your forgiveness, a body broken out of our Savior's love for us, and a body (the church) united in allegiance to its Lord.

B. Prayer

Father, as we remember Your Son in the loaf and cup, may You lead our hearts in joyful obedience toward Your throne of glory. We pray in the name of the one who died for us, amen.

C. Thought to Remember

Sharing in the Lord's Supper sustains our spirits.

Involvement Learning

Some of the activities below are also found in the helpful student book, Adult Bible Class. *Don't forget to download the free reproducible page from www.standardlesson.com to enhance your lesson!*

Into the Lesson

As learners arrive, give each a piece of red yarn that is 10" in length. Say, "Tie this in a loose bow on a finger. Keep it on until later in the class."

As class begins, summarize Joshua 2:1-13, then read Joshua 2:14-21. Comment: "That scarlet red cord became a mark that would tell the destroyers of Jericho, 'Pass over this house.' It was therefore similar to the blood marks the children of Israel had put over their doors in Egypt to escape God's avenging angel (Exodus 11, 12). Today we will use this red cord *[point to the one on your own finger]* to remind us of a Passover of greater significance: the one that directly preceded the crucifixion of Jesus, where His shed blood became the 'red stripe' that saves us from God's wrath."

Into the Word

Read today's text, Luke 22:14-30, aloud. Say, "Prepositions can be very significant. Let's see how." Prepare in advance four very large flash cards with the following prepositions, one each: *AMONG, BEFORE, UNTIL,* and *WITH.* As you show each word, ask, "What is the significance of this word as you see it in today's text?" This will encourage a close examination of the text; encourage free discussion. If your class is larger, you may wish to do this in small groups.

You should point out the following key concepts if learners do not do so. For *BEFORE,* Jesus notes this supper precedes His suffering (v. 15). For *UNTIL,* Jesus states what He will not do until fulfillment or coming of the kingdom of God (vv. 16-18). For *AMONG,* three matters may be noted: the cup and bread were shared among the group (vv. 17, 19), questions of betrayal and greatness occurred among the disciples (vv. 23, 24), and Jesus' response dealt with what it meant for Him to be among them (vv. 26, 27). For *WITH,* note that Judas's hand—the hand of the betrayer—was with that of Jesus on the table (v. 21).

As you move to discuss verses 24-27, distribute the "Who's the Greatest?" activity from the reproducible page, which you can download. This will highlight Jesus' utter superiority. You can do this as a whole-class response activity or have learners work in study pairs. Follow by asking two learners to read aloud Matthew 18:1-4 and Matthew 19:13, 14, one each. Then ask, "How could the 12 disciples dare argue about such an issue, especially considering the gravity of the occasion?" Discuss.

Option: Distribute copies of a facsimile "report card" with three subjects noted: (1) knowledge of the truth, (2) personal self-evaluation, and (3) spiritual progress. For each have the letter-grade *F* already assigned. Say, "The three *Fs* stand for 'Forgetting First Facts.' That was the disciples' mistake; it is often our mistake as well: we forget the basic facts of Jesus' sovereignty, we think more highly of ourselves than we should, and we end up looking like spiritual babies!" Discuss.

Into Life

Distribute copies of the "Eager" activity from the reproducible page, which you can download. This will get learners thinking about their level of enthusiasm for the things of the Spirit, including participation in the Lord's Supper. This can be a take-home activity if time is short.

Draw class attention back to the red yarn. Say, "Find a prominent place to hang this at home or work for the week ahead. Let it remind you daily that you are blessed indeed by the blood of Jesus."

Option: Prepare in advance "coins" made from lightweight cardboard. One side of the coins will carry the statement *I Am the Greatest!* The other side will say *Jesus Is the Greatest!* Give each learner a coin as you say, "This coin represents the choice to be made daily, but it's not a matter to be decided by a casual 'coin flip.' It is a matter of the will. Which side of the coin will you put up each day?"

March 31
Lesson 5

The Lord Lives

Devotional Reading: Luke 24:22-26
Background Scripture: Luke 24:1-35

Luke 24:13-21, 28-35

13 And, behold, two of them went that same day to a village called Emmaus, which was from Jerusalem about threescore furlongs.

14 And they talked together of all these things which had happened.

15 And it came to pass, that, while they communed together and reasoned, Jesus himself drew near, and went with them.

16 But their eyes were holden that they should not know him.

17 And he said unto them, What manner of communications are these that ye have one to another, as ye walk, and are sad?

18 And the one of them, whose name was Cleopas, answering said unto him, Art thou only a stranger in Jerusalem, and hast not known the things which are come to pass there in these days?

19 And he said unto them, What things? And they said unto him, Concerning Jesus of Nazareth, which was a prophet mighty in deed and word before God and all the people:

20 And how the chief priests and our rulers delivered him to be condemned to death, and have crucified him.

21 But we trusted that it had been he which should have redeemed Israel: and beside all this, to day is the third day since these things were done.

. . . .

28 And they drew nigh unto the village, whither they went: and he made as though he would have gone further.

29 But they constrained him, saying, Abide with us: for it is toward evening, and the day is far spent. And he went in to tarry with them.

30 And it came to pass, as he sat at meat with them, he took bread, and blessed it, and brake, and gave to them.

31 And their eyes were opened, and they knew him; and he vanished out of their sight.

32 And they said one to another, Did not our heart burn within us, while he talked with us by the way, and while he opened to us the scriptures?

33 And they rose up the same hour, and returned to Jerusalem, and found the eleven gathered together, and them that were with them,

34 Saying, The Lord is risen indeed, and hath appeared to Simon.

35 And they told what things were done in the way, and how he was known of them in breaking of bread.

Key Verse

And their eyes were opened, and they knew him; and he vanished out of their sight. —**Luke 24:31**

Undying Hope

Unit 2: Resurrection Hope

Lessons 4–9

Lesson Aims

After participating in this lesson, each student will be able to:

1. Retell the encounter between Jesus and the two disciples on the road to Emmaus.
2. Explain how the two disciples changed from seeing Jesus as having failed their hopes to be Redeemer of Israel to energizing their hope that He is Savior of the world.
3. Sing a hymn or chorus that celebrates the risen Lord.

Lesson Outline

Introduction

A. After the Funeral

In some traditions, a wake is held in the home of the deceased after a funeral. The body of the deceased is present in this ceremony, and food and drink are served to those who have come to pay their respects. In some churches, a meal is held in the church fellowship hall. But no matter what the tradition, everyone eventually goes home after a funeral. We cannot stay at the church, the funeral parlor, or the cemetery very long. We go home.

Jesus died less than 24 hours after He celebrated a Passover meal with His disciples. His body was buried late on a Friday afternoon, a rushed interment to beat the arrival of the Sabbath that began at sundown (John 19:31). The stunned disciples stayed together (John 20:19), but they shared sadness and shock more than food or drink. There had been no proper funeral for their friend and teacher.

The next day, Sunday, some of Jesus' disciples apparently did what we do after a funeral: they started for home. Two set out for Emmaus, a village outside Jerusalem. The unexpected turn that this trip took is the subject of this week's lesson.

B. Lesson Background

The Gospels highlight the role of the 12 apostles, but there were other followers of Jesus as well. We see this in the plurality of candidates available to replace Judas (Acts 1:23). The other, non-apostolic disciples included both men and women (see Luke 8:1-3). About 120 of them were gathered together in Jerusalem sometime between Jesus' resurrection and the Day of Pentecost (see Acts 1:15).

Our story today concerns two such disciples. The name of one is given as *Cleopas*. We have no other confirmable information about this man. But one intriguing suggestion is that he is the same as the *Cleophas* of John 19:25, mentioned as being the husband of one of the women named *Mary* who stood by the cross as Jesus died. That leads to the further theory that the other, unnamed disciple in today's lesson could be that Mary. If these two are husband and wife walking back to their home village of Emmaus in Luke 24:13, that would throw a certain light on today's story regarding the hospitality they offered to Jesus. But if (1) Mary the wife of Cleophas is the same as "Mary the mother of James," who had witnessed the empty tomb (Luke 24:10), and (2) Luke 24:22-24 establishes that the two disciples in today's text had not witnessed the empty tomb, then (3) the unnamed disciple of today's study would not be Mary the wife of Cleophas.

Jerusalem was the largest city in the region, perhaps 30,000–50,000 in population. It was surrounded by many small villages of a few hundred people each. The residents of these villages tended vineyards, fields, orchards, flocks, and herds. The temple city of Jerusalem was fed economically by these villagers, who traveled to Jerusalem several times a year for festivals and to pay an annual temple tax. Emmaus was one such village. Today we are uncertain of its actual site, since the village was likely destroyed in the Roman military campaign that swept through Palestine in AD 66–70.

I. Sad Walk

(Luke 24:13, 14)

A. Departing from Jerusalem (v. 13)

13. And, behold, two of them went that same day to a village called Emmaus, which was from Jerusalem about threescore furlongs.

Our story begins with two people leaving Jerusalem for nearby Emmaus. The phrase *of them* refers back to "the eleven and . . . all the rest" of Luke 24:9; thus these two are followers of Jesus. Their walk of *threescore furlongs* (about seven miles) will take them two or three hours. Luke does not say why the pair is going to Emmaus, but the likely reason is that they are returning home.

The phrase *that same day* refers us back to Luke 24:1, which discusses events on "the first day of the week" (compare Luke 24:21, 22). This is Sunday. Earlier that day, Mary Magdalene had led a group of women to Jesus' tomb in order to give His body a more fitting burial (Luke 23:55–24:10). They had found the tomb open and empty, being told by two angels that Jesus was risen from the dead.

This was reported to the apostles and others (Luke 24:9), but the report was met with general disbelief. Peter, however, went to check. He too found an empty tomb (24:11, 12).

B. Discussion on the Road (v. 14)

14. And they talked together of all these things which had happened.

The two disciples are talking freely, unconstrained by the atmosphere of fear in Jerusalem (compare John 20:19). They have much to talk about, given recent events! These include the triumphal entry of Jesus into Jerusalem, the controversial cleansing of the temple, Jesus' arrest and trials, the crucifixion and quick death of Jesus, His burial, and (especially) the reports of the empty tomb and angelic announcements of Jesus' resurrection. There certainly is a lot to talk about!

II. Stranger Joins

(Luke 24:15-21)

A. Concealed Identity (vv. 15, 16)

15. And it came to pass, that, while they communed together and reasoned, Jesus himself drew near, and went with them.

Luke pictures the two disciples engaged in heavy discussion. We are not told where Jesus comes from, and the two disciples seem too engrossed in conversation to notice. By the time they are aware of His presence, He is walking alongside them. It is not unusual in Jesus' day for unacquainted travelers to walk together and talk. This would be something like talking with a

HOW TO SAY IT

Cleopas	*Clee*-uh-pass.
Cleophas	*Klee*-o-fus.
Emmaus	Em-*may*-us.
Gorbachev	***Gore***-bah-*choff.*
Magdalene	*Mag*-duh-leen or Mag-duh-*lee*-nee.
Mikhail	Mih-kha-*ill.*
Nazareth	*Naz*-uh-reth.
Pentecost	*Pent*-ih-kost.
Sadducee	*Sad*-you-see.
Sanhedrin	*San*-huh-drun or San-*heed*-run.
Sergeyevich	Ser-*ghe*-yeh-vich.

fellow passenger during a plane flight today without expecting to see that person again.

16. But their eyes were holden that they should not know him.

This is an early spring day, so there is likely a chill in the air. The travelers perhaps are "bundled up" a bit, with facial features not easily seen. The failure of the two disciples to recognize Jesus is attributable to more than a scarf across the bottom half of His face, however. The fact that *their eyes were holden* indicates a divine prevention of recognizing Jesus until the proper time (compare Mark 16:12).

Grief-filled Walks and Talks

Assassinations form a dark thread in the tapestry of American history. Many of us are old enough to remember the assassinations of President John F. Kennedy in 1963, of Dr. Martin Luther King, Jr. in 1968, etc. We retain vivid mental images of such tragic days. Those were days of shock, disbelief, and grief. Many attempted to cope by talking through their anguish with others.

Jesus' walk with two disciples on the road to Emmaus was both similar to and different from those events. The sadness at the violent, unjust death of a leader was a similarity. Also similar was the shared anguish as the disciples talked through their grief. But one thing was very different: unbeknownst to those grieving disciples, their leader was alive and talking with them!

Grief is part of the human condition. But when we lift our grief to God in prayer, we do so in the name of our living leader, our living Lord! Because He lives, He is the one who ultimately dries all tears (Revelation 21:4). —C. R. B.

B. Questioned Conversation (v. 17)

17. And he said unto them, What manner of communications are these that ye have one to another, as ye walk, and are sad?

Whether by tone of voice or facial expression, Jesus notices the sadness of the two disciples. Perhaps their talking is punctuated by sobs of grief. We can also surmise that Jesus sees the deep sadness in their hearts (see John 2:25).

The question Jesus asks does not mean that He is trying to get information that He lacks. He already knows why they are sad. The question, rather, is intended to be a conversation starter.

What Do You Think?

If Jesus visited you this week, what would He most likely find you discussing?

Talking Points for Your Discussion

- Over lunch at work
- With family in the evenings
- While socializing with friends
- With fellow Christians after Sunday worship
- Other

C. Incredulous Response (v. 18)

18. And the one of them, whose name was Cleopas, answering said unto him, Art thou only a stranger in Jerusalem, and hast not known the things which are come to pass there in these days?

With the city walls of Jerusalem perhaps still in sight, the two disciples know that this stranger has also come from Jerusalem. It is therefore difficult for them to understand how He can be unaware of the stunning events of the past week. On the identity of Cleopas, see the Lesson Background.

D. Recounted Events (vv. 19-21)

19. And he said unto them, What things? And they said unto him, Concerning Jesus of Nazareth, which was a prophet mighty in deed and word before God and all the people.

Jesus is not mocking these two. Rather, He is drawing them into a conversation. Their reply to His question *What things?* gives us a four-point perspective regarding what at least some followers of Jesus believe about Him.

First, Jesus' background is known: He is from Nazareth, a village in Galilee (compare Luke 4:16). Jesus' opponents also are aware of this (Luke 4:34; John 19:19). Second, Jesus is understood to be a prophet (compare Matthew 21:11). This means that the people see Jesus as having been appointed by God to speak for God.

Third, Jesus has been *mighty in deed and word* (compare Acts 7:22). Jesus' reputation among the people has been built on both His miracles (Luke

7:21) and His powerful preaching (4:22). Fourth, Jesus' ministry has been done in the presence of *God and all the people.* These were not secret things, but have been accomplished in public, widely known (compare Acts 26:26).

What Do You Think?

How is the way you explain Jesus similar to and different from the way Cleopas explained Him?

Talking Points for Your Discussion

- Matthew 10:32, 33
- Acts 17:22-31
- 1 Corinthians 9:19-23
- 1 Peter 3:15

20. And how the chief priests and our rulers delivered him to be condemned to death, and have crucified him.

The chief priests are the temple elites from the Sadducee party. The *rulers* are the members of the Jewish high council, the Sanhedrin. How Jesus ended up on a Roman cross is not a mystery to the people. They realize that the Jewish masters of Jerusalem had collaborated with the Romans to secure Jesus' death. This is the big news that the stranger seems to have missed—the death of a prophet through the hands of their own religious leaders. We can detect in this response a note of dismay and awareness of injustice.

21. But we trusted that it had been he which should have redeemed Israel: and beside all this, to day is the third day since these things were done.

The first half of this verse reveals the biggest reason for the disciples' sadness. Above all, Jesus' death seems to have signaled an end to their hope of Jesus being the one chosen by God to lead their nation out of bondage (compare Luke 1:68; 2:38).

In all of this, Luke wants us to understand that although these two disciples hold a very high estimate of Jesus that is correct in many ways, they have missed the central aspect of what He has been doing. He did not come to redeem Israel politically, but to save people from the bondage of sin.

If seen in a political or nationalistic sense, the death of Jesus is a tragic end to such hopes. If seen according to the plan of God, though, Jesus' death is part of a strategy to bring salvation. It is necessary that Jesus' death be followed by His resurrection to show God's vindication (see Acts 2:31-36). The fact that *to day is the third day since these things were done* ties this conversation to Luke 24:1, 46.

What Do You Think?

When was a time for you that dashed hopes eventually resulted in something unexpected and ultimately better?

Talking Points for Your Discussion

- Regarding a health issue
- Regarding a family issue
- Regarding a church issue
- Regarding a relationship issue
- Other

III. Savior Reveals

(Luke 24:28-35)

A. Hospitality Extended (vv. 28, 29)

28, 29. And they drew nigh unto the village, whither they went: and he made as though he would have gone further. But they constrained him, saying, Abide with us: for it is toward evening, and the day is far spent. And he went in to tarry with them.

When the trio arrives at Emmaus, the two disciples have reached their destination. It is late afternoon, but Jesus (whose identity is still hidden) seems as if He is continuing on. Although unaware of the identity of this stranger, the two disciples extend Him hospitality. *Abide with us* is an invitation for a meal and a bed for the night.

We wonder what motivates the two to extend such hospitality (compare Judges 19:15-21). One clue may be found in the preceding verses of Luke 24:25-27 (not in today's text). There Luke tells us that this mysterious stranger has given the pair an in-depth lesson on the prophecies of Scripture concerning the Messiah. They want to hear more from this man, for the wheels are turning in their heads.

B. Bread Broken (vv. 30, 31)

30. And it came to pass, as he sat at meat with them, he took bread, and blessed it, and brake, and gave to them.

Visual for Lesson 5

Point to this visual as you introduce the discussion question associated with verse 32.

Some think that what happens here is reminiscent of the last supper (see Luke 22:19). At least two things work against this idea: Jesus' statement in Luke 22:16 (see last week's study) and the lack of any cup mentioned (compare 22:17, 20). Further, the blessing and breaking of bread was not a new thing at the last supper (see Matthew 14:19). Since the eyes of these two disciples are opened to recognize Jesus only after the blessing and breaking of bread (v. 31, next), they likely see something personally familiar in Jesus' actions.

31. And their eyes were opened, and they knew him; and he vanished out of their sight.

What happens now is completely unexpected. Whatever has been keeping the two disciples from recognizing Jesus is removed, and they now realize the risen Lord has been sitting right there with them! No sooner does this glorious realization dawn on these two than Jesus is gone. He does not merely duck into the shadows—He vanishes. Jesus' postresurrection appearances and disappearances have an aura of "suddenness" about them (compare Matthew 28:9; John 20:19, 26; 21:4).

Blindness and Change

K'hron Green was 15 years old when he lost his sight in May 2008 as a result of a car accident. He was sent to a rehabilitation facility in the Detroit area, where he was angry and defiant at first. But over the next three years, he became a mentor to others who had sustained traumatic brain injuries as he had. Green's physical eyes were effectively closed, but the eyes of his heart were opened. His speech therapist describes the change in his outlook on life as "just shy of a miracle."

Jesus' disciples suffered great trauma in seeing their leader killed. But that trauma wasn't what kept the disciples on the road to Emmaus from recognizing Jesus. Their "blindness" was from God, and it was He who lifted it.

The disciples' temporary blindness in this regard was accompanied by a spiritual blindness of mistaken expectations of what the Messiah was to accomplish. Jesus had to contend with this kind of blindness right up until His ascension (see Acts 1:6). But the one who opened the eyes of the physically blind (Luke 7:21, 22) still works to correct spiritual blindness. As He does so in our lives, may we be mentors to those who still need to "see" Jesus. —C. R. B.

C. Hearts Burned (v. 32)

32. And they said one to another, Did not our heart burn within us, while he talked with us by the way, and while he opened to us the scriptures?

Not only do the two disciples understand that Jesus is risen, they also are better able to interpret their experiences on the road with Jesus. They now realize why they had experienced a sensation described as a burning in the heart. At the time, they probably could explain that sensation only in terms of the marvelous Scripture lesson they were receiving from the stranger. But now they realize the supernatural cause: the presence of the risen Lord. They have been getting information from the best possible source!

What Do You Think?

What was an occasion when you had "a goose bump moment" regarding a sudden realization about Jesus?

Talking Points for Your Discussion

- During a time of personal Bible study
- During a sermon
- When sharing the gospel with another
- Other

D. Risen Lord Proclaimed (vv. 33-35)

33. And they rose up the same hour, and returned to Jerusalem, and found the eleven gathered together, and them that were with them.

These two disciples cannot wait until morning to share their experience. So they scurry back to Jerusalem, perhaps even arriving after dark. Their return must be surprising to the apostles who are gathered with other disciples, but not as surprising as the news the two from Emmaus are given even before they share their own experience.

> *What Do You Think?*
>
> When was a time you were convicted to do something "the same hour" of your conviction? How did things turn out?
>
> *Talking Points for Your Discussion*
>
> - Administering or receiving baptism (Acts 16:33)
> - Performing an act of benevolence
> - Confronting wrongdoing
> - Other

34. Saying, The Lord is risen indeed, and hath appeared to Simon.

The Greek sentence structure indicates that this is the report of those still in Jerusalem. Earlier that day, Simon Peter himself had encountered the risen Lord (see 1 Corinthians 15:5). Placed alongside Luke 24:36-39 (next week's lesson), what we see here is a mixture of belief and unbelief among the members of this core group. Any remaining doubts will be dispelled soon enough. The report we see here has been repeated every Easter, every Resurrection Sunday since: *The Lord is risen indeed!*

35. And they told what things were done in the way, and how he was known of them in breaking of bread.

Now the two disciples from Emmaus tell their own story. The fact that they relate the story from *what things were done in the way* to *how he was known of them in the breaking of bread* means that they do not leave anything out.

We should not expect to have a visual experience of the risen Christ today, nor is it necessary. We rest in His promise that "where two or three are gathered together in my name, there am I in the midst of them" (Matthew 18:20). As Simon Peter affirms many years later, "whom having not seen, ye love; in whom, though now ye see him not, yet believing, ye rejoice with joy unspeakable" (1 Peter 1:8). Hallelujah, He is risen indeed!

Conclusion

A. He Is Risen Indeed!

During the twentieth century, the Soviet Union was officially an atheist state where persecutions of Christians and the church were common. The final days of the Soviet Union witnessed a beginning of *glasnost* (meaning "openness") in that society, and some interesting things happened.

One of these took place during one of the last great May Day parades in Moscow. After the parade's seemingly endless procession of troops and military equipment, a small, ragtag group entered Red Square. The group consisted of shabbily dressed priests and other Christians—those who had felt the government's persecution firsthand. The leader carried a large cross, which he raised high as they approached the reviewing stand.

On the reviewing balcony was Mikhail Sergeyevich Gorbachev, the ruler of that Communist empire. The small group stopped in front of and below this powerful man and his entourage, the masters of millions of people. The huge crowd watched with interest, and a hush came over the people when the Christians stopped. The leader, holding the cross, raised his voice as he said, "Mikhail Sergeyevich, Christ is risen!"

In a world soaked with unbelief, this message never changes. Christ is risen from the dead. The world can never be the same because the Son of God has conquered death. May our hearts burn with the reality of the risen Lord!

B. Prayer

Father, Your Son is risen indeed! Help us to open eyes to see that fact. We pray this through the power of Jesus' precious name, amen.

C. Thought to Remember

Encounter the risen Christ again today.

INVOLVEMENT LEARNING

Some of the activities below are also found in the helpful student book, Adult Bible Class.
Don't forget to download the free reproducible page from www.standardlesson.com to enhance your lesson!

Into the Lesson

Before learners arrive, draw on the board a large time line with the following reference points: *Palm Sunday, Monday, Tuesday, Wednesday, Thursday, Friday, Saturday, Resurrection Sunday.* Give each learner a few index cards and a hymnal or other song book of Christian music. Say, "Find compositions with lyrics that depict one or more events of Jesus' final week. Write lines from your discoveries on the index cards, one entry per card."

As a group, discuss how the cards should be arranged on the time line; affix cards in the proper location as conclusions are reached. (You may wish to consult a final-week chronology in a Bible dictionary in advance.) Emphasize that while the story of the crucifixion and resurrection is familiar to many, it should never lose its significance in our lives.

Alternative: Place in chairs copies of the "Jesus' Final Week" activity from the reproducible page, which you can download, for learners to work on as they arrive. Your discussion of the results will serve as the transition to Into the Word.

Into the Word

Bring construction paper for five pairs or groups of three to have two sheets each. (Smaller classes can delete the assignment for Group 3.) Furnish each pair/group a handout with the following identical instructions: "Read your assigned verses and identify the emotions expressed or implied in the passage. Then draw faces that express those emotions, one emotion per face. Answer the questions posed." Below these common instructions, each handout will include one of the following sets of individualized instructions.

Group 1: Luke 24:13-17. What were the "all these things" (v. 14) that these disciples were discussing? What emotion or emotions do you think they were experiencing? Why? What happened that interrupted their intense conversation?

Group 2: Luke 24:18-21. What emotion or emotions do you think the disciples experienced as the result of Jesus' question in verse 17? Why? Does verse 21 indicate an additional emotion? If so, what was it?

Group 3: Luke 24:22-27. Although these verses are not part of the lesson text, they reveal that the two disciples had heard a report of the resurrection. What emotion did they seem to experience as they recalled that report? How do you think their emotions changed, if at all, as Jesus chided them and began to explain the Scriptures?

Group 4: Luke 24:28-31. What emotion did the two disciples reveal as they urged Jesus to stay with them? What did Jesus do that drew the disciples' reaction? What emotion do you think they experienced because of the way Jesus left them?

Group 5: Luke 24:32-35. What emotion did the disciples experience as Jesus talked with them about the Scriptures? What role do you think this emotion played in their decision to return to Jerusalem right away? What emotion might they have been feeling as they shared the story of their encounter with Jesus?

Give each group time to show the faces they have drawn and give brief explanations. Stress the point that there was a major transformation in their emotions once they realized Jesus was alive.

Into Life

Ask learners to share times when they were disappointed or in despair over unmet expectations, only to have their expectations exceeded by something else. What role did Christian faith (or lack of faith) play in all this?

Option 1: End the class with a time of praise and a prayer of thanks for the "exceeded expectations" we have in Christ. *Option 2:* End the class by having one of your musically gifted learners lead in singing some stanzas of a familiar hymn or song about the resurrection.

The Lord Appears

Devotional Reading: 1 Corinthians 15:1-8
Background Scripture: Luke 24:36-53

Luke 24:36-53

36 And as they thus spake, Jesus himself stood in the midst of them, and saith unto them, Peace be unto you.

37 But they were terrified and affrighted, and supposed that they had seen a spirit.

38 And he said unto them, Why are ye troubled? and why do thoughts arise in your hearts?

39 Behold my hands and my feet, that it is I myself: handle me, and see; for a spirit hath not flesh and bones, as ye see me have.

40 And when he had thus spoken, he shewed them his hands and his feet.

41 And while they yet believed not for joy, and wondered, he said unto them, Have ye here any meat?

42 And they gave him a piece of a broiled fish, and of an honeycomb.

43 And he took it, and did eat before them.

44 And he said unto them, These are the words which I spake unto you, while I was yet with you, that all things must be fulfilled, which were written in the law of Moses, and in the prophets, and in the psalms, concerning me.

45 Then opened he their understanding, that they might understand the scriptures,

46 And said unto them, Thus it is written, and thus it behooved Christ to suffer, and to rise from the dead the third day:

47 And that repentance and remission of sins should be preached in his name among all nations, beginning at Jerusalem.

48 And ye are witnesses of these things.

49 And, behold, I send the promise of my Father upon you: but tarry ye in the city of Jerusalem, until ye be endued with power from on high.

50 And he led them out as far as to Bethany, and he lifted up his hands, and blessed them.

51 And it came to pass, while he blessed them, he was parted from them, and carried up into heaven.

52 And they worshipped him, and returned to Jerusalem with great joy:

53 And were continually in the temple, praising and blessing God. Amen.

Key Verse

He said unto them, These are the words which I spake unto you, while I was yet with you, that all things must be fulfilled, which were written in the law of Moses, and in the prophets, and in the psalms, concerning me. —**Luke 24:44**

Photo: Design Pics / nPine / Valueline / Thinkstock

UNDYING HOPE

Unit 2: Resurrection Hope

LESSONS 4–9

LESSON AIMS

After participating in this lesson, each student will be able to:

1. List the points of evidence for believing in Jesus' resurrection.

2. Relate the importance of this evidence to the call to be witnesses for Christ.

3. Make a list of opportunities that he or she will have to be a witness for Christ in the next few weeks.

LESSON OUTLINE

Introduction

A. Where Does God Live?

Many parents have been challenged by a small child who asks innocently, "Where does God live?" Our answer may reflect a struggle to answer on the child's level. We might say, "God lives in our hearts," only to be met with a quizzical, "How?" We might say, "God lives in Heaven," only to be asked, "Where is Heaven?" We might say, "God lives in the church," only to have the child wonder which church in town that might be.

Where does God live? The problem with this question is that the one asking it may assume that God has a physical need to live somewhere, and our answers may reflect this. How we answer may be true in one sense but inaccurate in another sense at the same time.

Our desire to understand "where God lives" is addressed in today's lesson, which concerns the ascension of Jesus Christ. That was a dramatic moment unlike anything ever witnessed (with the possible exception of 2 Kings 2:11). Jesus did not rise from the dead to resume His earthly life and eventually die again. He rose to be with His disciples for a short time and then return to the Father.

B. Lesson Background

The ancients believed in an "up-down" universe. "Below" was the underworld that housed the dead; "above" was Heaven, the realm of celestial beings. When Jesus returned to the Father, He *ascended*—that is, He went up into the sky. Everyone who witnessed this would have understood that to be the proper way to reach Heaven (compare 2 Corinthians 12:2).

Even so, we know that there is no physical "place" in the sky (or anywhere else) where God lives because we understand the abode of God in a spiritual, nonspatial way, as Paul did (see Acts 17:24). Thus when reading of Jesus' ascension, we should not be sidetracked by trying to account for all of the physical characteristics of His departure.

What is important is to grasp the significance of Jesus' ascension and to remember His final words just before that event. In so doing, we share the faith of those who heard those words as confirmation that Jesus had been dead, had come back to life, and then underwent an amazing transition.

In last week's lesson, we saw Jesus joining in mysterious fashion two disciples on the way to Emmaus (Luke 24:15). He later disappeared from their sight after they recognized Him (24:31). These disciples returned to report their encounter to the larger group in Jerusalem (24:33). In today's lesson, Jesus appears to the disciples in a startling way.

I. Seeing Jesus
(Luke 24:36-43)

A. Startling Appearance (vv. 36, 37)

36, 37. And as they thus spake, Jesus himself stood in the midst of them, and saith unto them, Peace be unto you. But they were terrified and affrighted, and supposed that they had seen a spirit.

We are given the impression that this appearance of Jesus is sudden, and no further explanation of that fact is offered here. As we try to understand this, we can note a couple of things.

First, there is no sense that Jesus opens a door and walks into the room (compare John 20:19, with the detail given of a locked door). This is not depicted as Jesus walking through walls, but as the reality that walls and locked doors cannot keep the risen Lord from appearing in the room.

Second, we can see that Jesus' appearance is completely unexpected and startling. These disciples know for certain that Jesus had died, and to see Him standing among them causes shock and fear. They recognize Jesus immediately—that's the very reason for their terror! His identity is not hidden as it was in Luke 24:16 (last week's lesson).

Just two verses prior, the gathered disciples had affirmed that "the Lord is risen indeed" (last week's lesson). Thus we see a mixture of belief and unbelief when that statement is placed alongside the fact that the disciples now interpret His appearance to be that of a spirit (compare Matthew 14:26). The lingering unbelief of those gathered is about to be thoroughly dispelled.

Jesus' greeting *Peace be unto you* is not just a way of saying "Hello," but is intended to calm the fears of the disciples (compare John 20:19-21). He wants to bring peace to their hearts.

B. Challenged Belief (vv. 38-40)

38. And he said unto them, Why are ye troubled? and why do thoughts arise in your hearts?

Jesus does not ask His questions because He needs information that He lacks. He already knows why they are troubled. The questions are for the benefit of the disciples—they need to examine their own doubts, their own hearts. Their doubting hearts make them unwilling to trust what their eyes see. It is a critical moment, the line between belief and disbelief. Jesus fully intends to give the disciples cause to believe that He is risen from the dead so they will put their faith in Him, the risen Lord.

39, 40. Behold my hands and my feet, that it is I myself: handle me, and see; for a spirit hath not flesh and bones, as ye see me have. And when he had thus spoken, he shewed them his hands and his feet.

Jesus does not expect the disciples to trust their eyes alone, so He invites them to touch Him (compare John 20:25-27; 1 John 1:1). By examining His hands and feet, they can see the wounds from the nails used to fasten Him to the cross.

While the crucifixion narratives in the Gospels themselves do not describe Jesus specifically as being nailed to a wooden cross, the use of nails and the resulting puncture wounds are clearly in

Visual for Lesson 6. *Point to this visual as you ask, "What are times in your life when the promised presence of Christ of Matthew 28:20 seems most real?"*

mind here (compare John 20:25; Acts 2:23). The Romans sometimes tie their victims to crosses using ropes, but nails are also a common method to affix hands and feet. Jesus shows His hands and feet because they bear marks of recent nail wounds. This indicates that the apparent Jesus in the room is neither an imposter nor a spirit.

For Jesus to say that He has *flesh and bones* is not intended to give us great insights into the nature of His resurrected body. Rather, Jesus' simple intent is to demonstrate that He is physically present. It is in this light that the disciples are invited to view His body and touch it.

What Do You Think?

How should you react when someone claims to have seen Jesus either physically or as a disembodied spirit?

Talking Points for Your Discussion

- Luke 17:23, 24
- John 20:29
- Acts 9:27; 10:41; 23:11
- 1 Corinthians 9:1
- Revelation 1:7
- Other

C. Unmistakable Demonstration (vv. 41-43)

41. And while they yet believed not for joy, and wondered, he said unto them, Have ye here any meat?

Jesus, knowing that some still doubt, offers an even more substantive demonstration of His physical presence: He asks for food so that He can eat it while they watch. *Meat* is used here in an older sense of our English word to mean "food in general" (as opposed to drink). Jesus has shown in His ministry a certain disregard for food (Matthew 4:1-4; Luke 12:22, 29; John 4:31-34). Thus it is highly unlikely that Jesus asks for food merely to satisfy a sense of hunger. Rather, His request is intended to dispel any lingering doubts about the reality of His physical existence as the disciples watch Him eat.

Before we are too critical of these disciples, we should put ourselves in their place. Imagine that you saw a person die right before your eyes. Then you attended an open-casket funeral, after which you witnessed the casket being lowered into the ground and the grave being filled with dirt. Then you gather with others somewhere for a memorial meal. Over the course of time, some people show up claiming that the deceased is alive again—you're confused. Suddenly, the person whose body was buried appears in the living room and begins to talk with you. You would be hard pressed to understand immediately what is happening! That is what is going on with these disciples.

42, 43. And they gave him a piece of a broiled fish, and of an honeycomb. And he took it, and did eat before them.

Jesus' request is honored quickly. His eating proves He is no ghost. He is the real man they have followed for over three years, now risen from the dead. If He were merely an apparition or figment of their imaginations, the tomb would not be empty (Luke 24:3).

Seeing Ghosts?

People are fascinated with ghost stories. Witness the popularity as a tourist attraction of the 160-room Winchester Mystery House™ in San Jose, California. Some claim that visitors have experienced the presence of ghosts there hundreds of times. Many people visit in order to have just such an experience.

This house owes its quirks of construction to Sarah Winchester (1839–1922). She believed that her late husband, the inventor of the Winchester rifle, was cursed because of all the deaths caused by his invention. A spiritualist convinced her that she too was cursed and could escape only if she were involved in continuous construction on the house. She acted on that belief for decades.

Consulting the spirits of the dead was one of "the abominations" to ancient Israel (Deuteronomy 18:9-13). But Jesus did not stand in the midst of the disciples because they held a séance to "call Him up" (compare 1 Samuel 28). They weren't expecting Him at all! And Jesus appeared in bodily form, not as a spirit or apparition. Sarah Winchester may well have been delusional, but Jesus proved that the disciples were not. May we seek the living Jesus only. —C. R. B.

II. Understanding Scripture

(Luke 24:44-49)

A. Imperative (v. 44)

44. And he said unto them, These are the words which I spake unto you, while I was yet with you, that all things must be fulfilled, which were written in the law of Moses, and in the prophets, and in the psalms, concerning me.

When Jesus conversed with the two on the Emmaus road, "he expounded unto them in all the scriptures the things concerning himself" (Luke 24:27). Jesus' use of Scripture is now described a bit more fully, as He is said here to use *the psalms,* not mentioned in the Emmaus episode. His death had been horrific, but it was a fulfillment, not a thwarting, of God's plan.

Jesus' approach reflects the Jewish threefold division of their Scriptures (our Old Testament). *The law of Moses,* the first five books of the Bible, is also known today as the *Torah* (literally, "instruction"). *The prophets* are also known as the *Nevi'im* (which is merely the Hebrew word for "prophets"). *The psalms* are part of the third section, which is known as the *Ketuvim* (literally, "the writings").

Christian editions of the Old Testament have all the same books, but we arrange their order differently. Jesus' comments on this occasion and that of Luke 24:27 indicate the importance for Christians to study the Old Testament for a full understanding of the Messiah. The fact that the New Testament authors quote extensively from the Old Testament further establishes the importance of studying the Old Testament.

> *What Do You Think?*
>
> What improvements do you need to make in your study of the Old Testament?
>
> *Talking Points for Your Discussion*
>
> - In frequency of study
> - In depth of study

Of all the events recorded in the Bible, this may be the one for which we would most like to have been present. Imagine having the comfort of knowing from firsthand experience that Jesus is risen from the dead! Combine that with an opportunity to sit at the Master's feet and hear Him explain Scripture, how it applies to Him, and what is accomplished through His death, burial, and resurrection (compare John 20:9)—what earthly experience could top this?

B. Explanation (vv. 45, 46)

45, 46. Then opened he their understanding, that they might understand the scriptures, And said unto them, Thus it is written, and thus it behooved Christ to suffer, and to rise from the dead the third day.

There is no single passage in the Old Testament that includes all of what Jesus says here, so we should understand this to be a summary of several passages (see Isaiah 53:3-12; compare Acts 8:32-35). Jesus' understanding of the fulfillment of the three-day time frame regarding His death and resurrection draws on the experience of Jonah (see Matthew 12:40).

This is a crucial moment in history because the significance of Jesus' death will be lost if His disciples do not understood it themselves. Jesus' lingering for 40 days between His resurrection and ascension (Acts 1:3) serves both to prove that He is risen and to teach His disciples the meaning of His death and resurrection. The preaching of the church depends on these proofs and explanations.

Some students think this teaching occurs at a later time, immediately before Jesus' ascension (and within this viewpoint there is a debate regarding whether the transition begins here or at v. 44). In any case, we are reading some final instructions given by Jesus to His disciples before He leaves them to be with the Father.

HOW TO SAY IT

Bethany	*Beth*-uh-nee.
Emmaus	Em-*may*-us.
Jonah	*Jo*-nuh.
Ketuvim *(Hebrew)*	*Ket*-you-vim.
Messiah	Meh-*sigh*-uh.
Nevi'im *(Hebrew)*	*Neh*-vih-im.
Pentecost	*Pent*-ih-kost.
syncretism	***sin***-kreh-*tih*-zum.
Torah *(Hebrew)*	*Tor*-uh.

C. Commission (vv. 47, 48)

47, 48. And that repentance and remission of sins should be preached in his name among all nations, beginning at Jerusalem. And ye are witnesses of these things.

The coming of the Son of God into the human sphere is only one phase of God's plan. It was prophesied and therefore intended that Jesus should die and be resurrected, but this is not the end. The disciples are now witnesses who can testify about the resurrection. They are therefore commissioned by the risen Lord to begin the next phase: the preaching of repentance and the resulting *remission of sins* to *all nations* (compare Matthew 28:19, 20; 1 Timothy 3:16).

This is a key message that Luke wants his readers to hear. Faith must be shared, for the salvation of the world is at stake (compare Acts 1:8). Jesus saves the lost (Luke 19:10) as this message is spread.

These words are not simply for the disciples who are gathered to watch Jesus depart; these words are for us too. As we follow the biblical plan of salvation in accepting Jesus as our Lord, we become witnesses who are charged with spreading this good news.

What Do You Think?

How can your church better help people make a connection between the Easter story and their daily lives?

Talking Points for Your Discussion

- Special events
- Special studies or sermon series
- Through existing programs
- Other

D. Promise (v. 49)

49. And, behold, I send the promise of my Father upon you: but tarry ye in the city of Jerusalem, until ye be endued with power from on high.

Remember that the Gospel of Luke is the first volume of a two-volume set. The author intends us to read the next volume, Acts, where the promise of the verse before us is fulfilled (Acts 1:8; 2:1-4). The *power from on high* is the outpouring of God's Holy Spirit on the disciples. (This will be the focus of next week's lesson.)

What Do You Think?

Which promises of God most influence choices you make daily and for the future? Why?

Talking Points for Your Discussion

- Fulfilled promises
- Promises yet-to-be fulfilled

III. Worshipping Jesus

(Luke 24:50-53)

A. Dramatic Departure (vv. 50, 51)

50. And he led them out as far as to Bethany, and he lifted up his hands, and blessed them.

This particular Bethany is undoubtedly the one on the southeast flank of the Mount of Olives. This village was something of a headquarters for Jesus during His final week (Matthew 21:17; Mark 11:11, 12; John 12:1). It is the home of Lazarus, Mary, and Martha (John 11:18, 19).

John 11:18 specifies that the distance between Jerusalem and Bethany is "about fifteen furlongs," which equates to less than two miles. Acts 1:12 tells us that the disciples will return "unto Jerusalem from the mount called Olivet, which is from Jerusalem a sabbath day's journey," which is less than one mile. Putting these two ideas together lets us conclude that the trip toward Bethany ends up somewhere on the Mount of Olives. It is here that Jesus blesses His followers while lifting His hands to Heaven in the posture of prayer.

51. And it came to pass, while he blessed them, he was parted from them, and carried up into heaven.

While still pronouncing a blessing, Jesus is physically removed from the group. The description of Jesus' being *carried up into heaven* is further noted as being "taken up; and a cloud received him out of their sight" in Acts 1:9.

There is no description of anyone on this occasion being privileged to witness Jesus being exalted to "the right hand of God" (Acts 2:33). Stephen will be privileged to see that result as he dies (Acts 7:55, 56; compare Romans 8:34; Colossians 3:1; and Hebrews 10:12). Even so, Luke leaves no doubt that the disciples experience Jesus' ascension as a return to His Father in Heaven.

Lies, and Where Hope Lies

San Diego police discovered evidence of a mass suicide on March 26, 1997. The victims were members of the "Heaven's Gate" cult, founded by Marshall Applewhite and Bonnie Nettles. The pair had claimed to be the two witnesses mentioned in Revelation 11:3. Their belief system was a combination of Christian ideas, New Age philosophy, evolutionary theory, and science fiction.

The result of such syncretism was a conclusion that the earth would soon be destroyed, and the only way to survive was to leave earth immediately. Thus did Applewhite induce 38 of his followers to commit mass suicide with him so their souls could board a spacecraft thought to be behind the Hale-Bopp comet.

The world is still looking for a way to transcend the bonds of this life. Jesus' ascension into Heaven left His followers filled with hope that they too would someday go to be with Him (compare John 14:1-4). We share that hope because we trust Jesus, not the lies of false prophets such as Applewhite (compare 1 John 4:1). —C. R. B.

B. Joyous Reaction (vv. 52, 53)

52, 53. And they worshipped him, and returned to Jerusalem with great joy: and were continually in the temple, praising and blessing God. Amen.

The disciples' return to Jerusalem is also noted in Acts 1:12. Rather than express anything like disappointment at being abandoned, the mood of the disciples is that of joyous worship (compare John 14:28; 16:22).

The atmosphere of worship does not cease that day of return to Jerusalem since the disciples are *continually in the temple,* meaning every day. Daily gatherings at the temple are part of the practice of Jesus' followers after His ascension (Acts 2:46; 3:1; 5:20, 21). That massive edifice has many places available for congregating in its spacious courts.

Therefore we should not picture the disciples cowering uncertainly in hiding in the days between Jesus' ascension and the Day of Pentecost. This is not what Luke wants us to see. The reality of Jesus' resurrection and the implications of His return to the Father are now embraced fully by this group of disciples. They will wait, but it will be with joyous anticipation of what the future holds, for Jesus has promised to send a great gift of power to them.

What Do You Think?

What impact can and should Jesus' ascension have on your witness for Him?

Talking Points for Your Discussion

- Regarding relatives
- Regarding former church members who have "fallen away"
- Regarding coworkers
- Regarding unsaved friends
- Other

Conclusion

A. Where Did Jesus Go?

Where did Jesus go? He did not "go" anywhere in the sense of "not being here," for He is not far from us (see Acts 17:27; Hebrews 13:5). He did indeed go to the right hand of God, where He serves as our advocate and priest in Heaven (Hebrews 4:14–5:10; 8:1), but Jesus is also with us because this is what He promised (Matthew 28:20).

N. T. Wright has said, "Ascension doesn't mean absence . . . it means sovereignty." We serve a risen Lord, and we serve Him with joyous anticipation of His return. We serve our Savior by heeding His words and taking the message of forgiveness and grace to all the world. We serve the King of kings, the one who has an impact on our lives today, some 2,000 years after the Bethany event.

B. Prayer

Father, may we be obedient as we take Your Son's message to the world. May we be joyous in our service as we worship and praise You. May we be expectant in our waiting, for our deepest desire is to be with You forever. In Jesus' name, amen.

C. Thought to Remember

The risen Jesus is also the present Jesus.

Involvement Learning

Some of the activities below are also found in the helpful student book, Adult Bible Class.
Don't forget to download the free reproducible page from www.standardlesson.com to enhance your lesson!

Into the Lesson

Draw two columns on the board. Above one column write *Bible*; above the other write *People*. Ask learners to brainstorm what Scripture says about the "dwelling place" of God. Jot responses in the *Bible* column. Then ask learners what they've heard people say about "where God lives." Write these responses in the *People* column. Their observations can be from fellow believers, televangelists, children, ancient mythology, etc.

Compare the two lists. Discuss possible reasons for wrong ideas. Say, "Today's lesson focuses on one of the most crucial moments in history. Let's see how our understanding of the biblical text affects our witness for Christ."

Into the Word

Form learners into groups of no more than six, then distribute the following assignments. (Larger classes can form additional groups with duplicate assignments.) *Group 1:* List the actions of Jesus and the disciples' reactions in Luke 24:36-43. *Group 2:* Identify Jesus' explanations to the disciples in Luke 24:44-49. *Group 3:* List what the disciples saw and heard and how they responded to Jesus' instructions in Luke 24:50-53.

Ask groups to share their findings, which should include the following:

Group 1: Jesus stood in their midst (v. 36); disciples reacted with terror and fright (v. 37). Jesus asked the disciples why they reacted as they did (v. 38), showed them His hands and feet, offering to let them touch Him (vv. 39, 40); disciples reacted with joy and wonder (v. 41); Jesus asked for something to eat (v. 41); disciples gave Him some food (v. 42). Discuss the logical sequence of actions and reactions. Note that Jesus acted in ways to give the disciples time to adjust to His unexpected presence. Use the lesson commentary for verses 38-43 to help learners see the significance of accepting these unusual events.

Group 2: Jesus commenced His explanations once the disciples accepted the fact of His physical presence. What had happened was a fulfillment of Scripture, not a thwarted plan (v. 44); the intent of this plan was repentance and forgiveness of sins for everyone (vv. 45-47); the vehicle for moving the plan forward was the disciples, who would be empowered to do so (vv. 48, 49). Use the lesson commentary for verses 44-49 to establish how the resurrection was a key part of the plan for the redemption of the world.

Group 3: The disciples heard and saw Jesus blessing them (v. 50); they saw Jesus carried up into Heaven (v. 51); they worshipped Him (v. 52); they obeyed by returning to Jerusalem (v. 52); they exhibited great joy (v. 52); they went to the temple and praised God (v. 53). Discuss how the disciples not only accepted what Jesus told them, but enthusiastically embraced it.

Distribute copies of the "An Amazing Story" activity from the reproducible page, which you can download. Assign to the same three groups the three rows in the exercise, one row each. Say, "Think of additional objections that skeptics might raise." After several minutes, have someone from each group present the case for the skeptics, then have someone else give the biblical response.

Into Life

Say, "We have seen how Jesus presented evidence of His resurrection not just to the disciples but to generations to come. That evidence compelled the disciples to be witnesses of God's plan to the nations. How does that same evidence compel us to be witnesses of that plan as well?" Discuss. Then have learners record names of people with whom they need to share the gospel. Follow with prayer for your learners' witness to them.

Alternative: Instead of the above, distribute copies of the "My Witness" activity from the reproducible page. Complete and discuss.

April 14
Lesson 7

The Lord Sends the Spirit

Devotional Reading: John 15:1-7
Background Scripture: Acts 2:1-41

Acts 2:1-16

1 And when the day of Pentecost was fully come, they were all with one accord in one place.

2 And suddenly there came a sound from heaven as of a rushing mighty wind, and it filled all the house where they were sitting.

3 And there appeared unto them cloven tongues like as of fire, and it sat upon each of them.

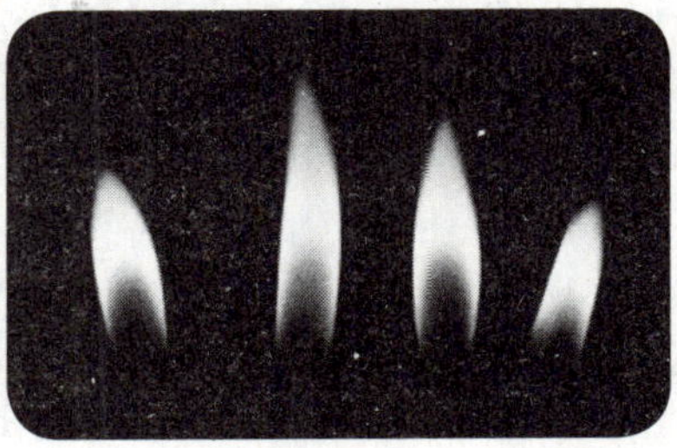

4 And they were all filled with the Holy Ghost, and began to speak with other tongues, as the Spirit gave them utterance.

5 And there were dwelling at Jerusalem Jews, devout men, out of every nation under heaven.

6 Now when this was noised abroad, the multitude came together, and were confounded, because that every man heard them speak in his own language.

7 And they were all amazed and marvelled, saying one to another, Behold, are not all these which speak Galilaeans?

8 And how hear we every man in our own tongue, wherein we were born?

9 Parthians, and Medes, and Elamites, and the dwellers in Mesopotamia, and in Judaea, and Cappadocia, in Pontus, and Asia,

10 Phrygia, and Pamphylia, in Egypt, and in the parts of Libya about Cyrene, and strangers of Rome, Jews and proselytes,

11 Cretes and Arabians, we do hear them speak in our tongues the wonderful works of God.

12 And they were all amazed, and were in doubt, saying one to another, What meaneth this?

13 Others mocking said, These men are full of new wine.

14 But Peter, standing up with the eleven, lifted up his voice, and said unto them, Ye men of Judaea, and all ye that dwell at Jerusalem, be this known unto you, and hearken to my words:

15 For these are not drunken, as ye suppose, seeing it is but the third hour of the day.

16 But this is that which was spoken by the prophet Joel.

Key Verse

They were all filled with the Holy Ghost, and began to speak with other tongues, as the Spirit gave them utterance. —**Acts 2:4**

Photo: Elizabeth Hachem / Lifesize / Thinkstock

Undying Hope

Unit 2: Resurrection Hope

Lessons 4–9

Lesson Aims

After participating in this lesson, each student will be able to:

1. Describe what happened leading up to Peter's dramatic sermon on the Day of Pentecost.

2. Explain how the unusual events of that day helped convince the God-fearing Jews who were present that the message of the apostles came from God.

3. Suggest some ways to get people's attention today as an open door to evangelism.

Lesson Outline

Introduction

A. The Ruined Vacation

Have you ever had a vacation ruined by an ugly incident? an accident or illness? a car breakdown? being victimized by a thief? bad news from home? I have friends who were happily vacationing in New York City on 9/11. Needless to say, their vacation was ruined.

Early first-century Jerusalem was full of visitors every spring. They were Jewish pilgrims from all over the Mediterranean world who came for the great Passover celebration and stayed until Pentecost, roughly two months later. This was like a religious vacation. In the year of today's lesson text (probably AD 30), the vacation of these visitors was disrupted. A visiting rabbi, named Jesus, was at first greeted by joyous crowds in a festive atmosphere. But things turned ugly. The visiting rabbi was in conflict with the Jewish authorities. The conflict escalated to the point that He was seized, given quick trials, and executed. It must have left a bad taste in everyone's mouth.

Coming seven weeks after Passover, the Feast of Pentecost was the end-event for most of these visitors. They would have begun to disperse the following week. That year, they might have left with this murderous memory weighing heavily on their hearts, a once-in-a-lifetime vacation ruined. But God, in His wisdom, did not let these pilgrims leave Jerusalem before experiencing an astounding event. The result was the birth of the church.

B. Lesson Background

The ancient Jewish calendar of special days had a great sense of history to it. One of the most important days on the calendar was Passover. That was a time to remember when God's angel of death "passed over" the Jewish households in Egypt that had been marked with the blood of a Passover lamb (Exodus 11 and 12). This feast day is connected with the exodus of the nation of Israel from Egypt, from their lives of slavery. Thus, Passover had the flavor of a day of national independence, something like America's Fourth of July. The single-day Passover celebration occurred in conjunction with the seven-day Feast of Unleavened Bread (Leviticus 23:5, 6). Thus these two came to be seen functionally as one celebration.

Pentecost, also called the Feast of Weeks, came seven weeks plus one day later (compare Exodus 34:22; Leviticus 23:15-21; Deuteronomy 16:9, 10). This length of time computes to 50 days, and *Pentecost* is a Greek word that simply means "fiftieth day." Today's lesson takes us to the first Day of Pentecost after Jesus' resurrection.

I. Disciples Energized

(Acts 2:1-4)

A. Long-Awaited Day (v. 1)

1. And when the day of Pentecost was fully come, they were all with one accord in one place.

Since Pentecost is 50 days after the Passover Sabbath, that means it falls on the first day of the week, Sunday. Jesus had lingered on earth for 40 days following His resurrection (Acts 1:3), so there is a period of less than two weeks between Jesus' ascension and this Pentecost day.

The mention of *all . . . in one place* leads us to investigate who is included in this "all." The group of disciples in Jerusalem at this time includes 11 of the 12 original apostles (Acts 1:13), the mother and brothers of Jesus (1:14), plus others for a total of about 120 (1:15). While waiting, they have taken care of at least one piece of vital business: choosing a replacement for Judas Iscariot to reconstitute the apostles to be 12 in number (1:15-26).

The gathering this particular morning seems according to the pattern the group has been following for several days. Acts 1:4-8 provides a promise that something profound is about to happen.

We don't know where the *one place* is. It could be the house of Mary, the mother of John Mark (see Acts 12:12). It may also be the place where the last supper had been celebrated, "a large upper room" (Luke 22:12; compare Acts 1:13). It may be in the temple courts outdoors. Wherever it is, it is large enough to accommodate 120 people.

> *What Do You Think?*
>
> How should the modern church celebrate the Day of Pentecost as the day of the church's birth, if at all?
>
> *Talking Points for Your Discussion*
>
> - Low-key observances
> - High-visibility observances

B. Attention-Grabbing Phenomena (vv. 2, 3)

2. And suddenly there came a sound from heaven as of a rushing mighty wind, and it filled all the house where they were sitting.

The first sign that this is a special day is auditory: a noise like *a rushing mighty wind.* We should notice that there is no mention of an actual wind blowing things about, but only the *sound* of a wind. This by itself is understood as a supernatural sign—a loud noise recognizable to be like the wind, but with no accompanying air movement.

3. And there appeared unto them cloven tongues like as of fire, and it sat upon each of them.

As the first phenomenon is wind-like sound without mention of moving air, the second phenomenon is a fire-like display without mention of heat. The description *cloven* seems to indicate a fire-like image that divides, with a tongue resting on each person. These are not fiery replicas of human tongues, but flame-like extensions of the fire.

C. Spirit-Given Speech (v. 4)

4. And they were all filled with the Holy Ghost, and began to speak with other tongues, as the Spirit gave them utterance.

The third phenomenon is the greatest of all. We might call it a combination of the fire/tongues and

HOW TO SAY IT

Cappadocia	Kap-uh-*doe*-shuh.
Diaspora	Dee-*as*-puh-ruh.
Elamites	*Ee*-luh-mites.
Euphrates	You-*fray*-teez.
Galilaeans	Gal-uh-*lee*-unz.
Mesopotamia	*Mes*-uh-puh-***tay***-me-uh.
Pamphylia	Pam-*fill*-ee-uh.
Parthians	*Par*-thee-unz (*th* as in *thin*).
Phrygia	*Frij*-e-uh.
proselytes	*prahss*-uh-lights.
Tigris	*Tie*-griss.

the wind/spirit (vv. 2, 3, above) as the gathered disciples begin to speak *with other tongues, as the Spirit* enables them. The tongues are known languages (see vv. 6, 8, below), but unlearned by the disciples.

Luke, the author, describes this as happening when the disciples are *all filled with the Holy Ghost* (compare Acts 4:31). To be *filled* in this sense is to be "controlled." This does not mean that the disciples have lost all personal control, becoming zombies of some kind. Rather, it means that the ability to speak in the unlearned languages is coming from a source outside themselves: the Holy Spirit (see also Acts 10:44-46). This is a miracle!

This is fulfillment of John the Baptist's promise "he shall baptize you with the Holy Ghost" (Matthew 3:11; Luke 3:16; compare Acts 1:5). The word *wind* is closely related to the word *spirit* (or *ghost*) in the Greek language, as both are understood to be invisible but real forces.

What Do You Think?

How has God worked in your church in unexpected but nonmiraculous ways? How does this strengthen your faith?

Talking Points for Your Discussion

- In the birth of your church
- During moments of crisis and change
- In extending its outreach
- Other

II. Visitors Confounded

(Acts 2:5-13)

A. Many Languages (vv. 5-11)

5. And there were dwelling at Jerusalem Jews, devout men, out of every nation under heaven.

The author briefly changes focus. In so doing, he sets the scene for the next surprising developments by reminding us that Jerusalem is full of foreign Jews at this time. Most of these are in town temporarily, having come for the Passover-through-Pentecost season of temple observances. Many will be headed home shortly (see the Lesson Background).

Luke's comment that they are from *every nation under heaven* is a testimony to the presence of Jews from across the Roman Empire. Such Jews are referred to as *the Diaspora,* meaning the dispersed nation of Israel (see John 7:35; James 1:1; compare Acts 21:21). We will get more details regarding the makeup of this international group in verses 9, 10, below.

What Do You Think?

What experiences have helped you most to appreciate the "every nation" nature of God's kingdom? Why?

Talking Points for Your Discussion

- At your church
- While on mission trips
- At Christian conventions
- Other

6, 7. Now when this was noised abroad, the multitude came together, and were confounded, because that every man heard them speak in his own language. And they were all amazed and marvelled, saying one to another, Behold, are not all these which speak Galilaeans?

This Holy Spirit–inspired speaking in other tongues begins to draw a crowd. These visiting Jews probably are fluent in Greek. It is likely that they are fluent in Hebrew as well according to Acts 22:2 (which probably refers also to a Day of Pentecost, per Acts 20:16). They could expect to hear one of these two languages on the lips of Galileans, but certainly not their mother tongues!

The question *Behold, are not all these which speak Galilaeans?* is disparaging. Whether because of the speakers' dress or accent (compare Matthew 26:73), the foreign Jews know that the ones speaking are from the rural area to the north. Galilee is part of the ancient territory of Israel, but at this time is a separate Roman district ruled by Herod Antipas (see Luke 3:1). The Jews of Galilee are considered uneducated and unsophisticated (compare Acts 4:13). Thus there is real surprise to witness people from that area as masters of many languages.

8. And how hear we every man in our own tongue, wherein we were born?

Because of the wide range of cities from which these Jews come (vv. 9-11, below), it is possible that there are very few representatives of certain languages in the multitude. Yet each person hears his or her local language being spoken! This is something they do not expect to hear until they return home.

9a. Parthians, and Medes, and Elamites, and the dwellers in Mesopotamia.

Luke now lists some of the regions represented. He begins with regions east of Jerusalem that are generally outside Roman control. We know from the Old Testament that many Jews remained in the east long after the return of Jews to Judea in 538 BC when many were released from captivity (Ezra 1, etc.).

The primary rival to the Romans is the Parthian Empire to the east. It controls the territory that encompasses the Parthians, Medes, and Elamites. These ancient peoples are located in what is modern Iran.

The Greek word *Mesopotamia* means "between the rivers," referring to the area between the Tigris and Euphrates Rivers. This territory is often called *Babylon* in the Bible; it is part of modern-day Iraq. This area is also controlled by the Parthians in the first century AD.

9b, 10a. And in Judaea, and Cappadocia, in Pontus, and Asia, Phrygia, and Pamphylia.

Next comes a listing of the easternmost provinces of the Roman Empire. Judea is the region around Jerusalem, and naturally there are many Judeans in this crowd. Cappadocia, Pontus, Asia, Phrygia, and Pamphylia are all areas in modern Turkey. Several of these areas are visited by the apostle Paul during his missionary journeys.

10b. In Egypt, and in the parts of Libya about Cyrene.

The third grouping consists of areas located in what we consider to be the northern part of Africa. These make up the southern provinces of the Roman Empire. We remember that the man forced to carry Jesus' cross was from Cyrene (Luke 23:26; compare Acts 13:1).

10c. And strangers of Rome, Jews and proselytes.

The *strangers of Rome* are subdivided into two groups: Jews and proselytes. There is a large Jewish population in the city of Rome and in other cities of southern Italy at this time. These Roman/Italian Jews are active in seeking converts *(proselytes)* to Judaism. So what the author is saying here is that the Roman Jews in Jerusalem on this day are represented by traditional Jewish families as well as by Gentiles who have converted to the Jewish faith.

There are three requirements for a Gentile man converting to Judaism: circumcision, a ritual bath, and the offering of a sacrifice at the temple. Some of these proselytes may be in Jerusalem at this time to complete the third requirement.

11. Cretes and Arabians, we do hear them speak in our tongues the wonderful works of God.

We now come to the last two people groups named. Those of the first are from the island of Crete, which has a sizable Jewish population. Crete is a prosperous center of trade because of its strategic location in the Mediterranean Sea. Arabians are Jews from the desert regions to the south of Jerusalem, especially from the Sinai peninsula and the northwest parts of the Arabian peninsula.

This verse gives us insight into the content of the marvelous speaking that is coming from the disciples as inspired by the Holy Spirit. The proclamation of *the wonderful works of God* is the language of praise. This is adoration of the Lord for His mighty works of creation and for His providential care (see Psalm 71:19; compare Luke 1:49; Revelation 15:3).

Babel Reversed

Pioneer Bible Translators and Wycliffe are two organizations dedicated to providing the people groups of the world with the Bible in their native languages. By one estimate, there are more than 6,900 spoken languages in the world today, with more than 30 percent of these not having any part of the Bible yet translated.

This tells us two things. First, there is still a lot of work to do before each and every people-group can have the gospel in its own language. Second, God did a very thorough job when He confounded the language of the people at Babel in Genesis 11!

When we contrast God's actions at confounding languages in Genesis 11 with the Holy Spirit's empowering on the Day of Pentecost, we see God drawing the peoples of the world back together. He wasn't giving back to people a common spoken language, but rather the message of a one-and-only Savior.

The miracle of enabling the disciples to speak in various languages was part of the proof. Now, some 2,000 years later, God is still drawing people to His Son through the gospel by means of the common spiritual language of *love* (John 3:16). We might call this "Babel reversed." What part will you play in God's plan? —C. R. B.

B. Mixed Reaction (vv. 12, 13)

12, 13. And they were all amazed, and were in doubt, saying one to another, What meaneth this? Others mocking said, These men are full of new wine.

When Luke tells us that a crowd is amazed or astonished, it generally means that the people are confused about something they have just witnessed because it does not square with their normal expectations (examples: Luke 2:47, 48; Acts 9:21). They have no reasonable explanation, so they begin to doubt. They suspect trickery. This is an attitude we see in the crowd on this Day of Pentecost in Jerusalem.

This spirit of doubt results in the conclusion by some that those who are speaking are drunk. To be drunk in public is scandalous behavior, so this accusation is strongly demeaning.

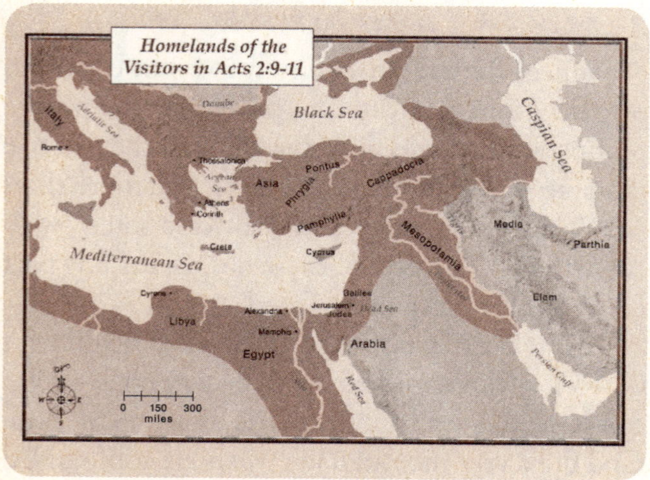

Visual for Lesson 7. *As you discuss verses 9-11, ask, "How can our church best respond to the increasing diversity of our country today?"*

> *What Do You Think?*
> What are some ways that people scoff at God's work today? How should you respond?
> *Talking Points for Your Discussion*
> - Acts 13:40, 41; 23:6-8
> - 1 Corinthians 4:12, 13
> - 2 Corinthians 5:11, 12
> - Colossians 4:6
> - 1 Peter 3:15
> - 2 Peter 3:3, 4

III. Peter Emboldened
(Acts 2:14-16)

A. Explanation Offered (vv. 14, 15)

14a. But Peter, standing up with the eleven, lifted up his voice, and said unto them.

Peter comes forward as the spokesman for the group, as he did in the selection process of a new apostle (Acts 1:15). Peter is portrayed in the Gospels as a strong personality prone to making mistakes (compare also Galatians 2:11-13). But having been reinstated personally by Jesus (John 21:15-17), Peter's boldness now is better directed.

> *What Do You Think?*
> When did you do something for God that you never pictured yourself doing? How did things turn out?
> *Talking Points for Your Discussion*
> - Public witness
> - Counseling situation
> - Evangelistic opportunity
> - Benevolence opportunity
> - Other

14b, 15. Ye men of Judaea, and all ye that dwell at Jerusalem, be this known unto you, and hearken to my words: for these are not drunken, as ye suppose, seeing it is but the third hour of the day.

The disciples' speaking in foreign tongues probably ceases to allow Peter to have the undivided attention of the gathered people. Appealing to common sense, Peter begins by refuting the insulting charge that the disciples are drunk. It is only *the third hour of the day,* which is about 9:00 AM. While there might be the rare person here or there who begins drinking wine immediately on arising, this would not be the case with a group such as the one the crowd is witnessing. Furthermore, drunkenness cannot explain what the crowd is experiencing. Inebriation does not lead to extraordinary language skills—quite the opposite!

B. Prophecy Fulfilled (v. 16)

16. But this is that which was spoken by the prophet Joel.

Last week's lesson considered the final words of Jesus in teaching the disciples that His death and resurrection were part of the plan of God as prophesied in Scripture. Peter now extends this idea to include the Pentecost phenomena. Not only was what happened to Jesus foreseen centuries before by God's prophets, so also was this outpouring of God's Holy Spirit foreseen.

Fulfillment of prophecy is not complete with Jesus' ascension; fulfillment continues among the works of the apostles in the first-century church. This sets the stage for Peter's marvelous sermon, based on the book of Joel and other Old Testament texts. The result of this sermon is the beginning of the church.

Flawed Vessels

Peter was a flawed vessel, presented in the Gospels as a man given to rashness. To human thinking, he seems an unlikely person to be chosen by God to preach the first gospel sermon, the sermon that established the church! But this was not the last time that God would work through a flawed individual to advance His plan. It has happened many times in the church's history.

One of the better known examples is that of John Newton (1725–1807). Newton spent his early life at sea, eventually becoming involved in the slave trade. But Newton underwent a spiritual conversion during a storm at sea in 1748. In time, he became an Anglican priest (1764), published his now-famous hymn "Amazing Grace" (1779), and wrote forcefully against the slave trade (1788).

Both Peter and John Newton continued to be flawed vessels long after they encountered Jesus, but God's grace worked to change those two. How is God working to change you? Where are you resisting God's changes? —C. R. B.

Conclusion

A. The Comforter Has Come

The account of that glorious Day of Pentecost has at least three abiding lessons for us. First, we recognize that the Holy Spirit has come to the church as part of the new covenant. The Old Testament certainly knows of God's Holy Spirit, but there is no sense there that the Spirit is a gift given to all the people of God. The coming of the Holy Spirit was foreseen by the Old Testament prophets and was promised by Jesus (John 14:15-26). The presence of the Holy Spirit is a primary difference between the people of God in the Old Testament and New Testament eras.

Second, we see that the Holy Spirit does not come passively, but with power. Many Christians today are uncomfortable talking about any sense of supernatural power from the Holy Spirit. They are missing a blessing. This doesn't mean that every Christian should be speaking in tongues, etc. (see 1 Corinthians 12:30). But it does mean that every Christian has the blessed gift of God's presence.

Third, Peter's bold speech shows us that the Holy Spirit empowers the preaching of the gospel. The display of tongues on the Day of Pentecost showed the diverse Jewish crowd that God was active in their midst. It set the stage for Peter to preach the entire gospel message. There is still power in the message that exceeds that of the messenger. When we share the gospel faithfully, God's Spirit is active in the reception of the message. This is true whether preaching from a pulpit or sharing with a friend.

B. Prayer

O Lord, may the presence of Your indwelling Spirit empower our worship, our love for You, and our sharing of the gospel. In Jesus' name, amen.

C. Thought to Remember

The coming of the Holy Spirit
changes everything.

Involvement Learning

Some of the activities below are also found in the helpful student book, Adult Bible Class. *Don't forget to download the free reproducible page from www.standardlesson.com to enhance your lesson!*

Into the Lesson

Have learners share times when something they had planned went wrong (examples: a ruined vacation, a botched surprise party, or stolen Christmas presents). Discuss how they felt and what they did to try and rectify the problem. Using the information from the lesson introduction, move learners from their own experiences to how the visitors to Jerusalem must have felt about the crucifixion of Jesus during Passover. Say, "Sometimes God has to change our perspective in order to get our attention. In today's lesson we will again see how God used extraordinary means to accomplish His purpose."

Ask learners what they know about the meaning and significance of the Passover and Pentecost observances. If responses reveal deficiencies in knowledge, use the Lesson Background to fill in the gaps.

Into the Word

Have a volunteer read Acts 2:1-4. Ask, "What are the extraordinary events that these verses mention? Why are these events important?" Jot responses on the board, but do not evaluate the correctness of the suggestions at this point—just list them.

Next, have a volunteer read Acts 2:5-11. Ask, "What is noteworthy in these verses? What could be the reason or reasons for the stated facts of these verses?" Jot responses on the board. Again, do not evaluate the correctness of the suggestions at this point.

Next, read Acts 2:12 but make no comment. (You'll come back to this verse later.) Finally, have someone read Acts 2:13-16. As before, ask learners to brainstorm the significance of these verses while you jot their unevaluated responses on the board.

Return to the class's earlier musings regarding the rationale for events noted in verses 1-4 and the significance of the facts noted in verses 5-11. Use the lesson commentary for these two sections to correct misconceptions and to answer questions the learners may have.

Use the results of this discussion to answer the question of verse 12: "What meaneth this?" Guide learners to the realization that God uses extraordinary means in Scripture to catch people's attention as He establishes that He is the source of what is happening. For today's lesson text, this helped the people recognize that the extraordinary things they were witnessing validated Peter's message of verses 14 and following as being from God and helped set aside the resistance of verse 13. Be sure to stress that what happened in today's text was nothing less than the birth of the church.

Option: Distribute copies of the "Not Your Typical Sunday Morning" activity from the reproducible page, which you can download. Have learners form study pairs to complete the activity. Encourage learners not to look at the suggested answers, but to see what they can recall from the study just completed. Allow sharing of conclusions, expecting some variety.

Into Life

Say, "As we think about the events surrounding the gospel sermon that accompanied the birth of the church, which parts can and should we expect to replicate in evangelistic sermons and messages today? Which parts should we not expect to replicate?" Expect responses that revolve around "attention getting" from miraculous and non-miraculous angles.

Alternative: Distribute copies of the "Attention! Attention!—The Right Way" activity from the reproducible page. Form learners into small groups to complete this exercise. Have groups share their ideas with the class as a whole. Try to achieve consensus on the two best ideas, given the context of the community where your church is located. Tell the class that you will present those two ideas to your church's leadership, and do so.

The Lord Will Return

Devotional Reading: Psalm 38:9-15
Background Scripture: 1 Thessalonians 4:13–5:11

1 Thessalonians 4:13-18

13 But I would not have you to be ignorant, brethren, concerning them which are asleep, that ye sorrow not, even as others which have no hope.

14 For if we believe that Jesus died and rose again, even so them also which sleep in Jesus will God bring with him.

15 For this we say unto you by the word of the Lord, that we which are alive and remain unto the coming of the Lord shall not prevent them which are asleep.

16 For the Lord himself shall descend from heaven with a shout, with the voice of the archangel, and with the trump of God: and the dead in Christ shall rise first:

17 Then we which are alive and remain shall be caught up together with them in the clouds, to meet the Lord in the air: and so shall we ever be with the Lord.

18 Wherefore comfort one another with these words.

1 Thessalonians 5:1-11

1 But of the times and the seasons, brethren, ye have no need that I write unto you.

2 For yourselves know perfectly that the day of the Lord so cometh as a thief in the night.

3 For when they shall say, Peace and safety; then sudden destruction cometh upon them, as travail upon a woman with child; and they shall not escape.

4 But ye, brethren, are not in darkness, that that day should overtake you as a thief.

5 Ye are all the children of light, and the children of the day: we are not of the night, nor of darkness.

6 Therefore let us not sleep, as do others; but let us watch and be sober.

7 For they that sleep sleep in the night; and they that be drunken are drunken in the night.

8 But let us, who are of the day, be sober, putting on the breastplate of faith and love; and for an helmet, the hope of salvation.

9 For God hath not appointed us to wrath, but to obtain salvation by our Lord Jesus Christ,

10 Who died for us, that, whether we wake or sleep, we should live together with him.

11 Wherefore comfort yourselves together, and edify one another, even as also ye do.

Key Verse

God hath not appointed us to wrath, but to obtain salvation by our Lord Jesus Christ.

—1 Thessalonians 5:9

UNDYING HOPE

Unit 2: Resurrection Hope

LESSONS 4–9

LESSON AIMS

After participating in this lesson, each student will be able to:

1. Tell what will happen to believers—both those who have died and those who remain alive—when Christ returns.
2. Contrast the lifestyles of the children of the day with the children of darkness.
3. Write a prayer of encouragement based on the hope of resurrection.

LESSON OUTLINE

Introduction
- A. Famous Returns
- B. Lesson Background

I. About Ignorance (1 THESSALONIANS 4:13-18)
- A. Status (vv. 13-15)
- B. Sequence (vv. 16, 17)
  - *Much Room, No Divorce*
- C. Support (v. 18)

II. About Times (1 THESSALONIANS 5:1-5)
- A. Thief in the Night (vv. 1-3)
  - *Where We Have a Choice*
- B. People of the Day (vv. 4, 5)

III. About Behavior (1 THESSALONIANS 5:6-11)
- A. What to Do (vv. 6-8)
- B. Why to Do It (vv. 9, 10)
- C. How to Interact (v. 11)

Conclusion
- A. Living Encouragements
- B. Prayer
- C. Thought to Remember

Introduction

A. Famous Returns

Julius Caesar returned to Rome in 49 BC as a victorious general, having extended the territory of the Romans to the North Sea. During World War II, General Douglas MacArthur returned triumphantly to the Philippines with a strong military force, having been forced to flee to Australia two years earlier. After his arrival he uttered the famous words, "I have returned." In 1979, Ruhollah Khomeini returned to Iran from his exile in Paris to lead a revolution. He became the Supreme Leader of the Islamic Republic of Iran.

Caesar, MacArthur, and Khomeini were heroes to some and villains to others. Such is the nature of history, for the triumphant return of a powerful leader can disrupt the power structures already in place. Caesar's return resulted in civil war, with Caesar eventually emerging as the master of the empire. MacArthur's return was the beginning of the end for Japanese occupation of the Philippines. Khomeini's return caused a revolt against the remnants of the previous regime, with opposition brutally suppressed.

The Bible tells us about the return of a leader who is perfectly just, unrivaled in power, and fully blessed by God. To be sure, there will be some who will rue the day of His return, for it will not be good news for "the powers that be" that have rejected Him. His return will not signal a new era in human history, but the end of history as we know it. This is the return in power and glory of the risen Lord, Jesus Christ, the Son of God.

B. Lesson Background

The return of Jesus is also called *the second coming* or *the Parousia*. It is referred to in 21 of the 27 New Testament books (absent only in Galatians, Ephesians, 1 Timothy, Philemon, 2 John, and 3 John). This teaching was an integral part of the preaching of Paul, and it was eagerly received by the churches he planted.

One such church was located in the city of Thessalonica. Paul was able to spend only about three weeks there (see Acts 17:1-10), and after his departure certain misunderstandings arose in the

Thessalonian church concerning Christ's return. The lessons for this week and next week will look at two letters Paul wrote to that church to correct wrong perceptions.

I. About Ignorance

(1 Thessalonians 4:13-18)

A. Status (vv. 13-15)

13. But I would not have you to be ignorant, brethren, concerning them which are asleep, that ye sorrow not, even as others which have no hope.

Paul's teaching among the Thessalonians perhaps has created great excitement and anticipation for the second coming of Jesus. As a result, these believers eagerly look for the Lord's return. However, a complication arises when some in their fellowship die. Working backward from Paul's response to the Thessalonians' unstated question, we easily can imagine that this situation has created a concern that these dead friends have missed out on Christ's return.

Paul always lives and preaches as if the Lord's return is imminent. He teaches his churches the great prayer of anticipation, "Maranatha!" which means, "Come, Lord!" (1 Corinthians 16:22; compare Revelation 22:20). The Thessalonians seem to be caught between this expectation and the present reality of death.

Paul's response is to chide his readers gently, warning that they are acting like nonbelievers, who *have no hope.* These are the ones who are without Christ (see Ephesians 2:12). The death of a beloved fellow Christian is certainly sad. But there should be no worry about the fate and status of that dead person.

We can note in passing that sleep is a common figure of speech in the Bible for death (examples: John 11:11-13; Acts 13:36). This does not require us to accept a theory of "soul sleep," the idea that human souls are in an unconscious state between death and resurrection. Although full details of what happens to people after death are not given in the Bible, there is no expectation of a period of unawareness between our deaths and our future existence beyond death (compare Luke 16:22-31).

What Do You Think?

How have you seen unbelievers express grief? How can this be a witnessing opportunity?

Talking Points for Your Discussion

- Where comfort is sought
- How death is discussed
- How the future is discussed
- Other

14. For if we believe that Jesus died and rose again, even so them also which sleep in Jesus will God bring with him.

The Christian understanding of the resurrection of men and women is built on the fact of Jesus' resurrection (see Romans 6:5). Jesus is the "firstfruits" of our own resurrection from the dead (1 Corinthians 15:20). This means that Christ's victory over death is a new reality that paves the way for the general resurrection of those who die. Paul understands that it is nonsensical to preach the resurrection of Christ if we do not see this as a harbinger of our own resurrections (1 Corinthians 15:12-16).

What Do You Think?

What helps you most in being certain that Jesus rose from the dead? Why?

Talking Points for Your Discussion

- Jesus' own words
- Descriptions of the future (1 Corinthians 15; Revelation; etc.)
- The martyrdom of the apostles
- Other

15. For this we say unto you by the word of the Lord, that we which are alive and remain unto the coming of the Lord shall not prevent them which are asleep.

Paul's statement *by the word of the Lord* means that what Paul is about to say is as ironclad as it can be: those who die before Christ comes again will not miss out. But Paul also introduces a relative element by the use of the word *prevent.* Today, we use this word to mean "to keep something from happening," but when the *King James Version* was first published the word *prevent* meant "to go or arrive before." Thus Paul's meaning is something like "those who are still alive when the Lord comes back will not go ahead of the others who are already dead." Any mourning for deceased Christians therefore should not be based on fear and regret that their deaths will cause them to be left behind when Christ returns.

B. Sequence (vv. 16, 17)

16. For the Lord himself shall descend from heaven with a shout, with the voice of the archangel, and with the trump of God: and the dead in Christ shall rise first.

Paul briefly describes what will happen when Christ returns, a sequence of events. This is definitely a physical description, not some fuzzy, spiritualized scenario. Christ himself will be seen coming out of the sky. This will be a supernatural appearance, for Revelation 1:7 tells us that "every eye" will witness this event. It will not be blocked by the earth so that those in, say, England are able to see Christ while those in Australia are not.

The Lord's descent will be heralded by three loud, supernatural noises. The first is *a shout.* Paul's word is a military term, giving the sense of a shout of victory. The second noise will be *the voice of the archangel,* signaling that Christ will return with an angel army (see Matthew 24:30, 31; 2 Thessalonians 1:7). This will be accompanied by the blast of *the trump of God* (think "trumpet"). This signals the participation of God himself (1 Corinthians 15:52). We can assume these three mighty sounds will be heard universally, waking all who are asleep (dead) and startling those who are alive.

Visual for Lesson 8. *As you discuss verse 16, point to this visual and ask, "Would you like to have this inscribed on your tombstone? Why, or why not?"*

Christ will come to take His people home. Those who are dead (like those who are the subject of concern for the Thessalonians) will be resurrected, coming back to life with new bodies. The fact that their resurrection comes *first* means it comes before what we see in the next verse.

17. Then we which are alive and remain shall be caught up together with them in the clouds, to meet the Lord in the air: and so shall we ever be with the Lord.

Having addressed the status and future of deceased Christians, Paul now discusses the issue of believers who are alive when Christ returns. Paul pictures the triumphant Lord above the earth, as if riding on the clouds (see Psalm 68:4). We can assume that the bodies of these still-living believers will be changed into immortal, resurrection bodies at that time, although Paul does not include that detail here (see 1 Corinthians 15:52). Thus there will be a great gathering of all God's people, living and dead.

The ascent of living people into the sky is sometimes called *the rapture.* The word *rapture* comes from the Latin translation of this verse and is reflected in the older English verb *rapt,* which once meant "to be snatched" or "to be caught up quickly." Many Christians give attention to theories of "the end times" that involve this term. Some scholars use a certain interpretation of *the rapture* to propose a sequence of end-time events.

Difficulties arise, however, when the picture of being *caught up* in the verse before us is integrated with ideas from other texts. The book of Revelation mentions a great tribulation, the revealing of the beast, the establishment of a 1,000-year (millennial) reign of Christ, etc. The difficulties involved in putting all these together in a time line cause some students to propose a "secret rapture," but that is not Paul's language.

Since interpretation of figurative language is uncertain at many points, there is room for disagreement regarding theories of the end times. This should not cause us to shy away from the Bible's teachings concerning the end times (called *eschatology*). What Scripture says in this area can be of great comfort to us.

Paul does not say here where the gathered multitude goes, simply that they will *ever be with the Lord.* In other passages, this final dwelling place is seen as Heaven (example: Revelation 7:9). We should remember that Paul's purpose here is not to give all the details of Christ's second coming, but to assure the Thessalonians that those who have died will not be left out.

Much Room, No Divorce

The so-called "wedding of the century" (the twentieth century, that is) took place on July 29, 1981, in London. A global audience of 750 million watched on TV as Lady Diana Frances Spencer was wed to Charles, Prince of Wales. Hundreds of thousands lined the streets to watch Diana's procession to the cathedral. It seemed that everyone wanted to be part of this "fairy-tale wedding"!

However, only 120 people were invited to the wedding dinner at Buckingham Palace after the ceremony. Sadder still, the fairy-tale wedding did not last. The marriage was in trouble within just a few years. Eventually, both Charles and Diana committed adultery. Formal separation was announced in 1992, followed by divorce in 1996 and Diana's tragic death in 1997.

Whether we are alive or not when Christ returns, none who are prepared for that event will have to worry about being left out of "the marriage supper of the Lamb" (Revelation 19:7-9). There will be room for everyone! There will be no possibility of adulterous affairs with false gods (contrast Jeremiah 3:6-9). The church need not worry about divorce from her bridegroom, Jesus. What a future we have! —C. R. B.

HOW TO SAY IT

Corinth	*Kor*-inth.
eschatology	ess-kuh-*tah*-luh-gee.
Julius Caesar	*Joo*-lee-us *See*-zer.
Maranatha *(Aramaic)*	Mah-ruh-*nay*-thuh.
Parousia *(Greek)*	Par-*oo*-see-uh.
Ruhollah Khomeini	Rue-*hoe*-lah Ko-*may*-nee.
Silas	*Sigh*-luss.
Thessalonians	*Thess*-uh-***lo***-nee-unz (*th* as in *thin*).
Thessalonica	*Thess*-uh-lo-***nye***-kuh (*th* as in *thin*).

C. Support (v. 18)

18. Wherefore comfort one another with these words.

This is Paul's main point. The Bible's teaching on the second coming of Christ can be confusing and disturbing for some. But it should not be so for believers, who trust Christ as Lord and look forward to His coming (compare Jude 21). We have not been abandoned by the risen Lord, for He will come to take us home (John 14:3).

What Do You Think?

How was your church a source of comfort to you when a loved one died?

Talking Points for Your Discussion

- Acts of service
- Funeral or memorial service
- Personal words of comfort
- Other

II. About Times

(1 Thessalonians 5:1-5)

A. Thief in the Night (vv. 1-3)

1, 2. But of the times and the seasons, brethren, ye have no need that I write unto you. For yourselves know perfectly that the day of the Lord so cometh as a thief in the night.

Paul realizes that his readers desire to know more specifics regarding the timing of Christ's return. Don't we all! This is not information they receive, though, for this will happen in the Father's undisclosed timing (see Matthew 24:36; Acts 1:6, 7). If we pay attention to this fact, we will appreciate the folly of setting dates for Christ's return. Our job is not to decipher prophecies to determine a plausible date, but to be ready always for His return. If Christ lingers until after our deaths, we must die ready. If we are alive at His return, we must live ready (see Matthew 24:44).

The comparison of Christ's second coming with that of *a thief in the night* emphasizes sudden arrival at an unexpected time. This comparison was made by Jesus himself (Matthew 24:43; compare 2 Peter 3:10; Revelation 3:3; 16:15).

Where We Have a Choice

Jim was "actively dying," as members of the health-care profession sometimes refer to conditions such as his. He was afflicted with multiple life-threatening ailments—chronic heart and lung problems, as well as spreading cancer. Any one of these conditions could take his life quickly, but he clung tenaciously to life.

Jim's doctors, nurses, social workers, and the hospice chaplain had prepared his family for his imminent demise, but Jim held on. He died only after his son, who lived overseas, was able to come and say good-bye. Such a scene takes place with surprising frequency: a dying person "chooses" the time of his or her death.

Jim's "choosing" was that only in a very limited sense, however. He would have died eventually even if he had stubbornly "chosen" not to. A mark of emotional and spiritual maturity is being able to recognize where we have choices and where we do not. We cannot choose the time of Christ's return, nor can we choose whether we shall be alive or not at that moment. What we *can* choose is whether that event will be a time of joyful celebration or tragic despair. —C. R. B.

3. For when they shall say, Peace and safety; then sudden destruction cometh upon them, as travail upon a woman with child; and they shall not escape.

Paul reminds us of the warnings of the prophets. Jeremiah warned people in his day not to believe the false prophets who proclaimed "Peace, peace; when there is no peace" (Jeremiah 6:14; 8:11; compare Ezekiel 13:10). Paul also invokes language from the warnings of Jesus that destruction will come on those who are not ready (Matthew 24:39; Luke 21:34-36), with an illustration of the suddenness of labor pains (see Mark 13:8).

B. People of the Day (vv. 4, 5)

4, 5. But ye, brethren, are not in darkness, that that day should overtake you as a thief. Ye are all the children of light, and the children of the day: we are not of the night, nor of darkness.

Paul reminds the Thessalonians that they have nothing to fear regarding the second coming of Christ. This should not lead to complacency, however, for Paul's readers are expected to be ready. As Paul notes in Romans 13:12, being ready involves casting off "the works of darkness" and putting on "the armour of light." *Children of light . . . day* behave differently from those *of the night . . . darkness* (compare Ephesians 5:8, 9).

This difference should be obvious. Christians have nothing to hide from God (1 John 1:5, 6; 2:28). Instead, we long deeply for Christ to come again so we might receive a "crown of righteousness" (2 Timothy 4:8). Paul has more to say about expected behavior in our next verse.

What Do You Think?

How does (or should) the anticipation of Jesus' return influence your response to troubling circumstances?

Talking Points for Your Discussion

- Political turmoil
- Financial ups and downs
- Health problems
- Other

III. About Behavior

(1 Thessalonians 5:6-11)

A. What to Do (vv. 6-8)

6, 7. Therefore let us not sleep, as do others; but let us watch and be sober. For they that sleep sleep in the night; and they that be drunken are drunken in the night.

Unlike Paul's explanation concerning the resurrection of the dead believers, this is probably material that the Thessalonians have heard before, since it speaks to everyday behavior. It bears repeating. Those who are ready for the Lord's return will *watch and be sober* as opposed to the unready who will be asleep and drunk (compare Luke 12:45). It is a mistake to sift the teachings of Jesus for exact details concerning His second coming and end up missing His main point: we must be alert and "Watch!" (Mark 13:37).

8. But let us, who are of the day, be sober, putting on the breastplate of faith and love; and for an helmet, the hope of salvation.

Many are familiar with Paul's description of spiritual armor in Ephesians 6:11-17. Since 1 Thessalonians is written 11 or so years before Ephesians, we detect that this is a favorite teaching of the apostle. Here Paul mentions the two most important defensive pieces of armor for a Roman soldier (compare Isaiah 59:17).

The mighty breastplate protects the chest, abdomen, and their vital organs. A spiritual breastplate is composed of *faith and love,* two sustaining Christian virtues (see 1 Corinthians 13:13). The helmet protects the head from blows that can cause instant death. Spiritually, such protection is *the hope of salvation,* the central message of this entire section. Christ's promised return is a cause for hope. Hope is so central to the Christian faith that Paul refers to the gospel message as "the hope of Israel" (Acts 28:20; compare Romans 8:24).

What Do You Think?

How does Paul's description of spiritual armor help you shine as a child "of the day"?

Talking Points for Your Discussion

- Regarding faith
- Regarding love
- Regarding hope

B. Why to Do It (vv. 9, 10)

9, 10. For God hath not appointed us to wrath, but to obtain salvation by our Lord Jesus Christ, who died for us, that, whether we wake or sleep, we should live together with him.

Closely connected with the second coming of Christ is the concept of final judgment. This judgment will be the justice of God delivered to sinners, here expressed as God's wrath. Part of Paul's message is that Jesus will deliver us from this wrath when He comes in glory (1 Thessalonians 1:10). As sinners, we deserve the anger of God (Romans 1:18; 3:23); salvation from this deserved wrath is offered to us by Jesus, our Savior (5:9).

Paul's picture of a wrathful God is not a popular topic today. We prefer the picture of a forgiving, loving God, the God of endless second chances and do-overs. Paul knows the loving side of God too (see Romans 5:8; compare Jeremiah 31:3). But Paul stresses that we must place our faith in Christ in order to escape God's wrath.

C. How to Interact (v. 11)

11. Wherefore comfort yourselves together, and edify one another, even as also ye do.

Paul ends this section by reminding the Thessalonians to use his words as mutual comfort. Paul (probably writing from Corinth) is not there to comfort them in person, and he does not need to be. They have the ability and the responsibility of building up one another. They can live as people of hope as they face the future.

Conclusion

A. Living Encouragements

The Christians in Thessalonica seem to have been a close-knit group. They depended on one another for support and encouragement. They had a close attachment to Paul and his coworkers (Silas, Timothy, and perhaps Luke). These men had brought a message of hope because salvation in Jesus Christ had come.

Sadly, the Thessalonians apparently had lost some in their fellowship to death after Paul's departure. This put hope to the test. Could the message of the gospel overcome the doubts of death? Paul's encouraging answer: those who die in Christ will not miss out on His blessed and glorious return.

In our age of overly privatized religion, we can miss an important part of Paul's message: the comfort we are to offer one another is based on our confidence in Christ's return. In this we become living encouragements.

B. Prayer

Father, may we never lose our hopeful anticipation of Your Son's return. May He find us ready. May He find us encouraging one another with His message of hope. In Jesus' name, amen.

C. Thought to Remember

Share comfort in the hope of Christ's return.

Involvement Learning

Some of the activities below are also found in the helpful student book, Adult Bible Class. *Don't forget to download the free reproducible page from www.standardlesson.com to enhance your lesson!*

Into the Lesson

Have the sentence fragment *In Heaven . . .* on the board as learners arrive. Give each an index card. Say, "Complete this sentence on your card." As learners finish, have them affix their cards to the board (provide masking tape). *Option:* Have playing a song that speaks about Heaven as learners complete their cards. (One possibility is "I Can Only Imagine" by MercyMe.)

Discuss some of your learners' ideas. Then say, "At His first coming, Christ sealed the promise of resurrection and Heaven for us; at His second coming, that promise becomes eternal reality. But the second coming also raises questions. Let's see how Paul addressed this issue for the Thessalonians."

Into the Word

Prepare three handouts with the following headings, one heading per handout: *Group 1: "Events of the Second Coming"—1 Thessalonians 4:13-18; Group 2: "Warnings/Comparisons"—1 Thessalonians 5:1-3;* and *Group 3: "Night vs. Day"—1 Thessalonians 5:4-11.*

Form learners into three groups, and give each a handout. Ask Group 1 to examine its passage and summarize the events associated with Jesus' second coming. Ask Group 2 to examine its passage to identify warnings and their respective comparisons. Ask Group 3 to examine its passage to identify contrasts between dark and light.

Preface Group 1's presentation by saying, "The Thessalonians seem to have been concerned that their deceased Christian friends would somehow miss out. How did Paul allay their fears?" *(Expected responses: Jesus will come out of the sky, there will be three loud noises, the dead will be resurrected, the living will be caught up to meet Jesus in the air, all who are in Christ will spend eternity with Him.)*

Preface Group 2's presentation by saying, "Paul didn't just write to answer the fears, but also to warn about those who weren't ready. What warnings did he give? To what did he compare those warnings?" *(Expected responses: No need to know times and dates / Jesus will come as thief in the night; sudden destruction and no escape / woman in labor.)*

Preface Group 3's presentation by saying, "Scripture offers several contrasts between those who will spend eternity with God and those who will not. Paul compared these two groups with light and darkness. What does he say in this regard?" *(Expected responses:* ***Night/Darkness****—surprised, asleep, unaware, drunk, suffers wrath;* ***Day/Light****—ready, sober, alert, clad with spiritual armor, encouraging one another.)*

Option: For extended study on the Night/Darkness and Day/Light contrast, distribute copies of the "Darkness and Light" activity from the reproducible page, which you can download. Have learners work in pairs. Allow time for discussion.

Close this segment by saying, "Paul's message is two-fold: some will spend eternity with God and some will not. Regarding the former, what should our response be?" *(encouragement)* "Regarding the latter, what should our response be?" *(evangelism)*

Into Life

Before class, make a list of names and addresses of your church's members who are elderly, shut-in, and/or terminally ill. Also bring Bible concordances as well as greeting cards that are appropriate for those on the list.

Say, "As a way to encourage some of our saints, I've brought some greeting cards we can send them. I'd like you to choose a name or two from the list and write a note of encouragement. Since Paul charged the Thessalonians to encourage one another with the promise of Jesus' return, include some verses that speak of Heaven." Learners can use the concordances to discover appropriate passages. Offer to mail the completed cards.

Alternative: Substitute the "Songs of Hope" activity from the reproducible page for the above.

The Lord Will Triumph

Devotional Reading: Titus 3:1-7
Background Scripture: 2 Thessalonians 2

2 Thessalonians 2:1-4, 8-17

1 Now we beseech you, brethren, by the coming of our Lord Jesus Christ, and by our gathering together unto him,

2 That ye be not soon shaken in mind, or be troubled, neither by spirit, nor by word, nor by letter as from us, as that the day of Christ is at hand.

3 Let no man deceive you by any means: for that day shall not come, except there come a falling away first, and that man of sin be revealed, the son of perdition;

4 Who opposeth and exalteth himself above all that is called God, or that is worshipped; so that he as God sitteth in the temple of God, shewing himself that he is God.

. . . .

8 And then shall that Wicked be revealed, whom the Lord shall consume with the spirit of his mouth, and shall destroy with the brightness of his coming:

9 Even him, whose coming is after the working of Satan with all power and signs and lying wonders,

10 And with all deceivableness of unrighteousness in them that perish; because they received not the love of the truth, that they might be saved.

11 And for this cause God shall send them strong delusion, that they should believe a lie:

12 That they all might be damned who believed not the truth, but had pleasure in unrighteousness.

13 But we are bound to give thanks alway to God for you, brethren beloved of the Lord, because God hath from the beginning chosen you to salvation through sanctification of the Spirit and belief of the truth:

14 Whereunto he called you by our gospel, to the obtaining of the glory of our Lord Jesus Christ.

15 Therefore, brethren, stand fast, and hold the traditions which ye have been taught, whether by word, or our epistle.

16 Now our Lord Jesus Christ himself, and God, even our Father, which hath loved us, and hath given us everlasting consolation and good hope through grace,

17 Comfort your hearts, and stablish you in every good word and work.

Key Verses

Now our Lord Jesus Christ himself, and God, even our Father, which hath loved us, and hath given us everlasting consolation and good hope through grace, comfort your hearts, and stablish you in every good word and work. —**2 Thessalonians 2:16, 17**

UNDYING HOPE

Unit 2: Resurrection Hope

LESSONS 4–9

LESSON AIMS

After participating in this lesson, each student will be able to:

1. Summarize Paul's argument that believers are to reject the deception of false teachers while remaining confident in the Lord's ultimate victory at His return.
2. Compare and contrast the deception in Paul's day with speculative teaching about "the end times" today.
3. Share with the class his or her best practices for avoiding evil deceptions.

LESSON OUTLINE

Introduction
- A. The Great Evil at the End
- B. Lesson Background

I. Unshaken Believers (2 THESSALONIANS 2:1-4)
- A. Day of Christ (vv. 1, 2)
  - *Using Discernment*
- B. Man of Sin (vv. 3, 4)

II. Deceived Believers (2 THESSALONIANS 2:8-12)
- A. Revealing of the Wicked (vv. 8-10)
- B. Sending of a Delusion (vv. 11, 12)

III. Chosen Believers (2 THESSALONIANS 2: 13-17)
- A. Glorious Christ (vv. 13, 14)
- B. Firm Traditions (v. 15)
  - *Traditions, Good and Bad*
- C. Encouraging Prayer (vv. 16, 17)

Conclusion
- A. Restraint, Rebellion, Reward
- B. Prayer
- C. Thought to Remember

Introduction

A. The Great Evil at the End

Once upon a time. These words signal the beginning of a fairy tale, a fanciful story of castles and kingdoms, dragons and princesses. We read these stories with certain expectations. Some of our favorites are full of tension, as when it seems Snow White will not wake from the poisoned apple or the prince will fail to find Cinderella. We are not surprised to hear of the craftiness and power of evil witches and wolves, but we would feel betrayed if the story ended with the bad guys winning.

The Bible has no fairy tales, but it does have a grand narrative about the end of time. We revel in the finale of this story: the triumphant return of the Lord Jesus Christ, addressed in last week's lesson. This week we will look at some other issues related to the end of time.

B. Lesson Background

The technical word for the field of Bible study that deals with end-time prophecies is *eschatology.* Daniel in the Old Testament and Revelation in the New Testament are used often as primary sources for information in this area. A number of Old Testament passages speak of the "day of the Lord" (examples: Isaiah 13:9; Ezekiel 30:3; Zephaniah 1:14). Many of these predict the destruction of the Jerusalem temple by the Babylonians (which happened in 586 BC), but there is often a sense of additional fulfillment beyond that catastrophic event.

Jesus himself spoke of events associated with the end of time, particularly in the Olivet Discourse (also called the Apocalyptic Discourse) in Matthew 24, 25; Mark 13; and Luke 21. We can see in Jesus' words certain predictions of the destruction of the temple in AD 70, but there are elements within the teaching that speak of the end of time as well. Jesus speaks of a period of great suffering that is followed by His own triumphant appearance (see Mark 13:24-26).

This great period of suffering and persecution is often called *the tribulation;* some scholars identify this as a well-defined period in the future that necessarily precedes the coming of the Lord. Several places in the New Testament speak about one or more figures who are to personify evil and opposition to the kingdom of God (see Revelation 13:1, 11; 16:13; 1 John 2:18, 22; 2 John 7). Paul's second letter to the church in Thessalonica, today's study, also discusses a figure of evil.

The letter of 2 Thessalonians begins with Paul offering support to Christians for the "persecutions and tribulations" they had been enduring (2 Thessalonians 1:4). Details of this persecution are not given. We can guess, however, that it may have involved pressure from the envious Jews of Acts 17:5, 13. They might have been upset with fellow Jews who had accepted Jesus as Messiah. The distress could have taken the form of social pressure, economic pressure, even physical intimidation (Acts 17:6).

I. Unshaken Believers

(2 Thessalonians 2:1-4)

A. Day of Christ (vv. 1, 2)

1. Now we beseech you, brethren, by the coming of our Lord Jesus Christ, and by our gathering together unto him.

Paul narrows his focus to details concerning Christ's return that are causing uncertainty within the congregation. He begins by summing up his teaching from the previous letter, that the Lord's return will result in a *gathering together unto him* of believers (compare 1 Thessalonians 4:13-17, last week's lesson).

HOW TO SAY IT

apocalyptic	uh-*pah*-kuh-***lip***-tik.
apostasy	uh-*pahs*-tuh-see.
Babylonians	Bab-ih-*low*-nee-unz.
Caligula	Kuh-*lig*-you-luh.
eschatology	ess-kuh-*tah*-luh-gee.
hyperbole	high-*per*-buh-lee.
Judas Iscariot	*Joo*-dus Iss-*care*-ee-ut.
Olivet	*Ol*-ih-vet.
Thessalonians	*Thess*-uh-***lo***-nee-unz (*th* as in *thin*).
Zephaniah	Zef-uh-*nye*-uh.

2. That ye be not soon shaken in mind, or be troubled, neither by spirit, nor by word, nor by letter as from us, as that the day of Christ is at hand.

Paul plunges into his discussion with a primary, reassuring point: the Thessalonians have nothing to fear regarding the timing of *the day of Christ.* Any teaching that proposes that Christ's return has already happened is false teaching. Paul warns that false teaching may come, perhaps by a letter that purports to be from him.

We know that Paul had sent Timothy (and perhaps others) to the believers in Thessalonica so they would have the advantage of clarifications from one or more of Paul's trusted assistants (see 1 Thessalonians 3:2, 6). Although this is a new church with no veteran Christians, they nonetheless have resources to protect against false teaching.

What Do You Think?

Thinking of the failed end-time prophecies of years gone by, how will you react to end-time prophecies you may hear in the years ahead?

Talking Points for Your Discussion

- *Left Behind* movies and books
- Harold Camping
- Mayan calendar
- Y2K
- 1 John 4:1

Using Discernment

Who hasn't received one of those e-mails from Nigeria that promises millions of dollars for helping with a monetary transaction? The details of the e-mails vary, but the theme is consistent: someone needs confidential assistance in making a money transfer, and you can help by providing your bank account information. After the millions are transferred into your account, you will be allowed to keep a certain percentage for your trouble.

This deception works because it appeals to a certain aspect of human nature. But those foolish enough to give out bank account numbers quickly discover that it is their own funds that end up being transferred! The FBI's Web site warns of numerous variations of this scam.

Paul warned the Thessalonians not to believe letters fraudulently claiming to have come from him. The frauds could be persuasive by appealing to what the Thessalonians "wanted" to be true. Even so, the frauds could be identified by their contradiction of what Paul preached or the letters he himself had written. The warning to the Thessalonians still applies! —C. R. B.

B. Man of Sin (vv. 3, 4)

3a. Let no man deceive you by any means: for that day shall not come, except there come a falling away first.

Paul believes throughout his ministry that the return of the Lord is near. But Paul also knows there will be some signs preceding the Lord's return (compare Luke 21:31). He introduces one such sign in this half-verse: *a falling away* (literally, "apostasy").

Paul is not specific about those who will fall away after believing in Christ for a while. This kind of news is troubling in any case, for we want to think that all of our Christian brothers and sisters will remain faithful to the end. But this is not the picture given in the New Testament (see Matthew 13:20, 21; 1 Timothy 4:1; 2 Timothy 4:10). An ongoing heartbreak for Christians is the abandonment of the faith by fellow believers.

What Do You Think?

What are some safeguards a church might use to help people avoid being deceived by false teachers?

Talking Points for Your Discussion

- In its Christian education ministry
- In its library or resource center
- In its constitution and/or bylaws
- In its small-group ministry
- Other

3b, 4. And that man of sin be revealed, the son of perdition; who opposeth and exalteth himself above all that is called God, or that is worshipped; so that he as God sitteth in the temple of God, shewing himself that he is God.

Another great sign preceding the Lord's return will be the rise and revealing of a powerfully evil person, pictured as having a worldwide impact. He will set himself up as a false god, a rival to the Lord God himself. This is portrayed dramatically as the deceiver going so far as to occupy *the temple of God.*

About a decade prior to Paul's writing here, the mad Roman Emperor Caligula ordered a pagan statue to be erected in the Jerusalem temple. Naturally, this created a crisis in Judea. Some students think that Paul is evoking images of that notorious incident as a "type" or "foreshadowing" of something that will happen in the future: the use of idolatrous things to pollute the holy things reserved for God. Others take this imagery to be part of a prophetic drama that requires the temple to be rebuilt in Jerusalem sometime after its destruction in AD 70 (which destruction is less than 20 years in the future as Paul writes) and then be desecrated by the evil person whom Paul describes.

Paul gives this evil person two descriptive titles. First, he is *that man of sin,* which points to someone who violates God's laws with impunity and arrogance. Second, Paul calls him *the son of perdition,* meaning the one whose future destruction is sure (compare Revelation 17:11). He will doubtlessly present himself like Paul's description of Satan as an "angel of light" (2 Corinthians 11:14). He is not a man of victory or triumph, however, but one who will be defeated, judged, and condemned (see 2 Peter 3:7).

What Do You Think?

What are some consequences of failing to discern satanic activities? How do we guard against this error?

Talking Points for Your Discussion

- In family life
- In politics
- In the church
- Other

We can note in passing that both the Greek and English wording for *the son of perdition* here exactly match the wording in John 17:12. But the reference there is to Judas Iscariot, who obviously is not the one Paul is talking about here. We can also note that the further description of this man as one who *exalteth himself above all that is called God* is similar to Daniel 11:36. But that passage refers to Antiochus IV, long dead by this point (see discussion in Lesson 3).

All this analysis can get very complicated! But before we get too wrapped up in this, we do well to keep Paul's intent in mind. Some Thessalonians are worried that "the day of Christ is at hand" (v. 2, above) or perhaps has already come and gone. Paul's correction is to say that that's not possible since a falling away and the revealing of a man of sin must happen first, and they haven't.

II. Deceived Believers

(2 Thessalonians 2:8-12)

A. Revealing of the Wicked (vv. 8-10)

8. And then shall that Wicked be revealed, whom the Lord shall consume with the spirit of his mouth, and shall destroy with the brightness of his coming.

Our lesson text skips over verses 5-7, but we should summarize what Paul says there: the person of evil being discussed is currently restrained. Yet there will come a time when this restraint is removed so that the final events may proceed in the plan of God. The removal of restraint on *that Wicked* person allows him to *be revealed,* to be out in the open. This will be followed by the Lord's coming, which will bring down the man of sin. The picture is one of instantaneous destruction.

The glorious coming of the Lord will overpower any and all opposition. The result is Jesus' unquestioned reign (see Matthew 25:31). If the power of evil is still at work in the world—and it is—then the Lord's coming has not yet happened.

9. Even him, whose coming is after the working of Satan with all power and signs and lying wonders.

Paul now explains that the source of this great wickedness is Satan. Does this mean that the "man of sin" is Satan himself? Or is Paul referring to two individuals—Satan and a man of sin who is in league with Satan? Scholars have argued for both positions. Either way, what we see here is a powerful pattern of deception (compare Matthew 24:24). The greatest of these lies is for this satanic figure to set himself up as if he were God (2 Thessalonians 2:4, above).

What Do You Think?

How have you seen the promise of Romans 8:28 fulfilled in various troubling situations?

Talking Points for Your Discussion

- When "good" people suffer
- When governments do things in opposition to God's law
- When church leaders behave sinfully
- Other

10. And with all deceivableness of unrighteousness in them that perish; because they received not the love of the truth, that they might be saved.

The tragic side of all this is that many will believe the lie and reject the truth. God does not want any to perish (2 Peter 3:9). But when the Lord Jesus comes again, there will be no more opportunities for switching allegiances to join the winning side. Those who have rejected Jesus will not be saved when He returns.

B. Sending of a Delusion (vv. 11, 12)

11, 12. And for this cause God shall send them strong delusion, that they should believe a lie: that they all might be damned who believed not the truth, but had pleasure in unrighteousness.

On the surface, these two verses are very challenging, for Paul seems to be saying that the ultimate source of deception is God himself—that God causes some to *believe a lie* and thus *be damned.* Yet we know that Satan, not God, is the great deceiver, the father of lies (John 8:44; compare 2 Corinthians 4:4). We also know that God doesn't tempt anyone with evil (James 1:13). How can we resolve the seeming contradiction?

A good rule in Bible study is to note what the surrounding statements say. This keeps things in context. In this case, verses 10 and 12 both contrast *truth* with *unrighteousness.* It is impossible to love both truth and evil at the same time. Those who reject God's truth end up embracing the deceptive nature of the pleasures of lawless wickedness. This in turn opens these unbelievers

Visual for Lesson 9

As you study verse 15, point to this visual and ask, "What challenges do you face in holding fast?"

to God's judgment since they have chosen to be deceived. They have already made up their minds. So when Paul says *God shall send them strong delusion,* he may be using the same kind of "God gave them up/over" conclusion that he uses in Romans 1:24, 26, 28. What we are seeing, then, is a declaration of God's judgment.

A second possibility is to see *God shall send them strong delusion* as hyperbole. For example, Luke 14:26 speaks of the need to "hate" family members when becoming a follower of Christ. But we do not expect literal hatred toward one's family members by Christians. If the text before us is to be taken as hyperbole as well, it means that God is still in control despite the activities of Satan and those in league with him. Thus *send them strong delusion* is taken to mean "permits them to be deceived." We can compare Job 1:12, where the Lord is said to permit Satan's testing of Job, with Job 2:3, where the Lord is said to be the one who acted in the testing.

III. Chosen Believers

(2 Thessalonians 2:13-17)

A. Glorious Christ (vv. 13, 14)

13. But we are bound to give thanks alway to God for you, brethren beloved of the Lord, because God hath from the beginning chosen you to salvation through sanctification of the Spirit and belief of the truth.

Paul now leaves the gruesome picture of the unbelievers' future to give thankful comfort to the Thessalonian believers. Paul is confident that they are not among the deceived. Because of their response to the gospel, they are among the chosen.

Paul gives several reasons for their hope of salvation. First, the Thessalonians are *beloved of the Lord.* Everything begins with God's love for us (John 3:16). Second, they have been sanctified (made holy) by the Holy Spirit. Third, God knows that they have a confident *belief of the truth.* As they hold fast to the things Paul has taught, their salvation is not in question. Holding fast means they won't be deceived by a "man of sin" figure.

14. Whereunto he called you by our gospel, to the obtaining of the glory of our Lord Jesus Christ.

Fourth, the Thessalonians have the hope of salvation because of the gospel. This is the good news that Jesus died for their sins, rose from the dead, and will return to gather all of His people (whether dead or alive at the time) to be with Him forever. This is the picture of *the glory of our Lord Jesus Christ,* a glory that all believers will have the privilege to witness and to share (1 John 3:2).

B. Firm Traditions (v. 15)

15. Therefore, brethren, stand fast, and hold the traditions which ye have been taught, whether by word, or our epistle.

Paul sums up this section with simple advice: just keep doing what you know to be right. The Thessalonians have been taught well (2 Thessalonians 2:5), even though Paul's stay with them was brief. They do not need to look for new teachings that will lead them astray. They have memories of Paul's preaching, and they now have two letters filled with doctrinal treasures to guide them as they continue to be lovers of the truth.

Traditions, Good and Bad

All my fathers have been churchmen,
Nineteen hundred years or so,
And to every new suggestion
They have always answered, "No!"

Isn't that how many churches function? Several years ago, a certain church almost split over the decision to begin a second Sunday service, which featured contemporary music and worship style. Some members left, but the church survived.

Then an interesting thing happened: the older, "traditional" service became less traditional, using visual media, singing some contemporary songs, and generally enjoying a new vitality. On the other hand, the newer, "contemporary" service, became locked into the format it had used from its inception. One church member who enjoys popping the balloons of pretense sometimes chides the "contemporary" folks by calling their service *traditional* and the "traditional" service *transitional.* His point is that the latter found freedom to adapt, while the contemporary worship became mired in its own set of traditions!

Paul admonished his Thessalonian readers to stay rooted in "the traditions which ye have been taught." By this he meant the apostles' instructions, not entrenched practices of human tradition. How can we make sure we distinguish between the two? —C. R. B.

C. Encouraging Prayer (vv. 16, 17)

16, 17. Now our Lord Jesus Christ himself, and God, even our Father, which hath loved us, and hath given us everlasting consolation and good hope through grace, comfort your hearts, and stablish you in every good word and work.

Paul ends this section with a prayer asking that God continue to safeguard the faith of the Thessalonians. There is unity between the Father and the Son (John 10:30), so there is a unified purpose in the strengthening and encouragement of these believers.

Worthy of note are the three "goods" Paul lifts up: *good hope, good word,* and *[good] work.* Paul has not taken up this much space in these two Thessalonian letters to address the second coming of the Lord simply to provide details for those fascinated by the intricacies of prophecy. Paul's purpose in teaching about Christ's return is to give his readers excellent expectations, a good hope concerning what the future holds. Having this hope should result is goodness in the believers' lives, whether in speech or deed. If our hope is in the Lord, our lives will bear His fruit.

What Do You Think?

How will your service for Christ this week be influenced by your expectation of His return?

Talking Points for Your Discussion

- In your witness at work or school
- In your faithfulness in worship and Bible study
- In your family relationships
- Other

Conclusion

A. Restraint, Rebellion, Reward

John Stott describes Paul's scenario in 2 Thessalonians 2 as "Restraint, Rebellion & Reward." For a time, the power of evil is restrained by God. At some point, this restraint is removed, with the result of rebellion among those who reject God's truth. This is followed by just and sure rewards from God. The wicked are punished, and those who have embraced the hope of the gospel are gathered to begin eternity with their risen Lord.

Throughout the history of the church, there have been those who have interpreted the events of their day as indicators of the Lord's soon return. This continues today. The modern interpreters may be as wrong as those of previous centuries, or they may be correct. Christ may return very soon, or He may delay for thousands of years. For believers, it does not matter. We have a blessed hope whether we live to see Christ return in power or are among the dead who are awakened by His call.

We should have no fear of "the man of sin," whoever he is, for we are among those who have washed our robes in the blood of the lamb. We will stand before God to worship and praise Him forever (Revelation 7:14-17).

B. Prayer

Lord God, may we continue to trust in You when evil gains power and when others reject the truth. May Paul's encouragement to the Thessalonians be ours as well. In Jesus' name, amen.

C. Thought to Remember

Celebrate Christ's past, present, and future victory.

INVOLVEMENT LEARNING

Some of the activities below are also found in the helpful student book, Adult Bible Class.
Don't forget to download the free reproducible page from www.standardlesson.com to enhance your lesson!

Into the Lesson

Option 1: Form learners into small groups to share beliefs about how and when Jesus will return, listing ideas on a piece of poster board. Read the remarks as you affix each poster to the wall.

Option 2: For a whole-class brainstorming activity, say, "Sometimes people predict dates for the Lord's return. What are some of these predictions, and who made them?" Jot responses on the board or ask a "scribe" to do so.

Say, "There are many ideas about how and when Jesus will come again. We find questions surfacing in the pages of the Bible on how and when this will happen. Our lesson text will show us how Paul encourages the church in Thessalonica about this issue."

Into the Word

Give each learner a handout with the heading "Discovering the Day of Christ." Include these instructions: "Today's passage, 2 Thessalonians 2:1-4, 8-17, is packed with information about the *who, what,* and *when* associated with 'the day of Christ.' Search the verses listed below, looking for information about this day; note that information beside the verse number." Have the following verse numbers listed vertically down the left side of the handout: 2, 3, 4, 8, 9, 10-12, 13, 14, 15, 16, 17. (Note: This activity may be done in pairs, in small groups, or as a whole class activity. If you do it in pairs or small groups, you can create two or more handouts with fewer verses each so the pairs or groups have different ranges of text to examine.)

As you discuss conclusions as a class, possible discoveries include the following: verse 2, don't believe false teaching that the day of Christ has already come; verses 3, 4, the day will be preceded by apostasy and the appearance of a "man of sin"; verse 8, the wicked one will be revealed and destroyed; verse 9, the wicked one will perform lying wonders; verse 13, believers are loved and sanctified; verse 14, believers will experience in some way the glory of Jesus; verse 15, believers must stand fast; verse 16, 17, God's love for believers gives comfort and hope.

Ask learners to turn their handouts over, draw a vertical line down the center, write "Wicked One" at the top of the left column and "Followers of Paul's Teachings" at the top of the right column. Say, "We now want to contrast the characteristics of the wicked one and of those who follow the gospel teaching of Paul. Take five minutes to scan the text and jot characteristics in the appropriate column." Review and discuss discoveries.

Tie the two activities together by asking, "How does satanic deceit make itself known in our culture today?

Option: Distribute copies of the "The End-Times News" activity from the reproducible page, which you can download. Ask learners to complete one of the three writing opportunities. Discuss results and compare with the lesson text.

Into Life

Say, "Truth and deceit are contrasted sharply in today's text. What are occasions in our daily routines where we may be challenged to ignore truths we've been taught about God and act in a manner contrary to that teaching?" Coax circumstances that reflect a variety of settings (as social events, work environments, parenting, private times when no one sees you, etc.).

As you jot ideas from a learner on the board, ask other class members, "What would you say to a Christian facing this situation that will encourage him or her to 'stand fast'?" After filling out the list, point to it as you ask, "Which of these is the highest-risk circumstance for you? You will not need to share your response here, but you need to identify it if you are going to 'stand fast.'" Form prayer teams to pray for each other's faithfulness when the deceiver attacks.

Living Hope

Devotional Reading: Lamentations 3:19-24
Background Scripture: 1 Peter 1

1 Peter 1:3-16

3 Blessed be the God and Father of our Lord Jesus Christ, which according to his abundant mercy hath begotten us again unto a lively hope by the resurrection of Jesus Christ from the dead,

4 To an inheritance incorruptible, and undefiled, and that fadeth not away, reserved in heaven for you,

5 Who are kept by the power of God through faith unto salvation ready to be revealed in the last time.

6 Wherein ye greatly rejoice, though now for a season, if need be, ye are in heaviness through manifold temptations:

7 That the trial of your faith, being much more precious than of gold that perisheth, though it be tried with fire, might be found unto praise and honour and glory at the appearing of Jesus Christ:

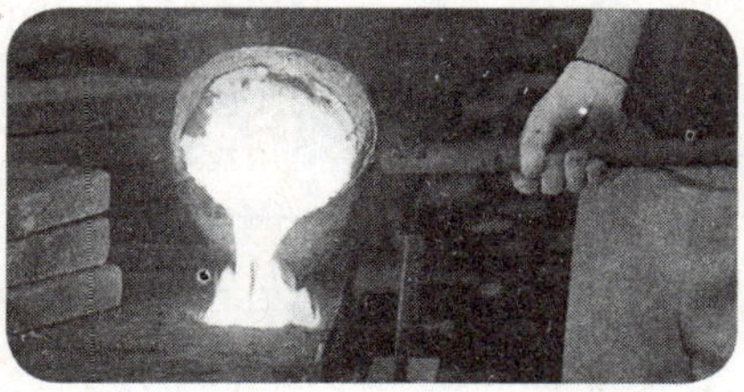

8 Whom having not seen, ye love; in whom, though now ye see him not, yet believing, ye rejoice with joy unspeakable and full of glory:

9 Receiving the end of your faith, even the salvation of your souls.

10 Of which salvation the prophets have enquired and searched diligently, who prophesied of the grace that should come unto you:

11 Searching what, or what manner of time the Spirit of Christ which was in them did signify, when it testified beforehand the sufferings of Christ, and the glory that should follow.

12 Unto whom it was revealed, that not unto themselves, but unto us they did minister the things, which are now reported unto you by them that have preached the gospel unto you with the Holy Ghost sent down from heaven; which things the angels desire to look into.

13 Wherefore gird up the loins of your mind, be sober, and hope to the end for the grace that is to be brought unto you at the revelation of Jesus Christ;

14 As obedient children, not fashioning yourselves according to the former lusts in your ignorance:

15 But as he which hath called you is holy, so be ye holy in all manner of conversation;

16 Because it is written, Be ye holy; for I am holy.

Key Verse

Blessed be the God and Father of our Lord Jesus Christ, which according to his abundant mercy hath begotten us again unto a lively hope by the resurrection of Jesus Christ from the dead. —**1 Peter 1:3**

Photo: Jupiterimages / Photos.com / Thinkstock

UNDYING HOPE

Unit 3: A Call to Holy Living

LESSONS 10–13

LESSON AIMS

After participating in this lesson, each student will be able to:

1. Tell what Peter says is the source, object, and expression of hope for the Christian.

2. Explain the relationship between personal holiness and salvation.

3. Identify one area of unholiness in his or her own life and make a plan for change.

LESSON OUTLINE

Introduction
- A. Wishes vs. Hope
- B. Lesson Background

I. Hope Founded (1 PETER 1:3-5)
- A. Basis (vv. 3, 4)
  - *Decay*
- B. Protection (v. 5)

II. Believers Refined (1 PETER 1:6-9)
- A. Trials, Value, Result (vv. 6, 7)
- B. Joy, Love, Goal (vv. 8, 9)

III. Plan Fulfilled (1 PETER 1:10-12)
- A. Prophets Had Searched (vv. 10, 11)
  - *Which Prophecies?*
- B. Answer Is Revealed (v. 12)

IV. Holiness Required (1 PETER 1:13-16)
- A. Results Expected (vv. 13-15)
- B. Reason Established (v. 16)

Conclusion
- A. Confident Expectation
- B. Prayer
- C. Thought to Remember

Introduction

A. Wishes vs. Hope

"I hope that the weather improves tomorrow." "I hope that the repairs on my car do not cost too much." "I hope that the home team has a good season this year." You probably have made statements like these at one time or another.

What do we mean when we say *hope* in these kinds of statements? We mean that there is one outcome that we prefer over another. We are expressing a wish. Such wishes may not be expressed with much confidence. They are what we *desire* to occur but not necessarily what we *expect.* It is easy to confuse the common usage of the word *hope* with the way that word is used in the New Testament. Today's study helps us avoid such confusion.

B. Lesson Background

Today's text comes from the first of the New Testament letters of the apostle Peter. As we learn from the letter's opening, Peter wrote to Christians in "Pontus, Galatia, Cappadocia, Asia and Bithynia" (1 Peter 1:1). These designations refer to an area that corresponds to modern Turkey. That region was controlled by Rome in Peter's day.

The Romans respected Judaism because of its antiquity. At first, the Romans viewed Christianity as merely an offshoot of Judaism, so the respect applied to Christians as well. But eventually the Romans came to see Christianity as a new religion in its own right. This created suspicion of Christians being "a class of men given to a new and mischievous superstition," as one ancient Roman historian put it in describing a Roman attitude during Nero's reign (AD 54–68).

Although the believers remained law-abiding citizens, they fell under suspicion of disorderly or criminal behavior, even insurrection against the government. Consequently, Christians in this region came under persecution. They faced insults, exclusion, loss of livelihood, arrest, and even violence. The churches of western Asia Minor were persecuted, suffering churches. The letter of 1 Peter, written about AD 64, addressed those Christians with a powerful reminder of the reality that lay beyond their suffering.

I. Hope Founded

(1 Peter 1:3-5)

A. Basis (vv. 3, 4)

3. Blessed be the God and Father of our Lord Jesus Christ, which according to his abundant mercy hath begotten us again unto a lively hope by the resurrection of Jesus Christ from the dead.

Letters in New Testament times usually start with a brief word of greeting and a statement of thanksgiving to a god. New Testament letters typically begin this way, with the thanks offered to the one true God. First Peter follows this common pattern, with the thanksgiving beginning here.

Note how many key ideas are contained in the beginning of this word of thanks. God is *Father,* a good and wise protector and provider for His people. He has the relationship of Father to Jesus, who himself is *Lord,* the divine ruler over all. Through Jesus we have received mercy, God's accepting us as friends and restraining our just punishment.

That mercy leads to our being *begotten* or born again. The expression "born again" in our time is widely taken to mean that one has had a dramatic conversion experience. Genuine conversion to faith in Jesus is often dramatic, but in its biblical usage that is not the emphasis of the expression. Instead, it stresses that through faith in Jesus one has a new family relationship. Under God's covenant with ancient Israel, one was "born" into His people. But in Christ anyone can be "reborn" into God's family. In fact, that is the only way one becomes part of God's family (John 3:3-8).

The result of this new family relationship is a new expectation of the future, a new hope. Like a family member with a sure inheritance, members of God's family can be confident of their future.

That hope can rightly be called *lively* (or "living") because it is founded on the triumph of life over death. Jesus' resurrection is the basis and guarantee for our future as believers in Him. Because God raised Jesus from the dead and because as believers we belong to Jesus, we have every reason for a confident hope that God will raise us up as well (1 Corinthians 15:20-23).

For all these reasons and more, Peter gives thanks to God. The term *blessed* when applied to God means to be worthy of praise and thanks.

What Do You Think?

Which Scripture passage(s) do you find most helpful in strengthening your "lively hope"? Why?

Talking Points for Your Discussion

- Acts 24:15
- Romans 15:13
- 2 Corinthians 3:10-12
- Hebrews 6:16-20
- Other

4. To an inheritance incorruptible, and undefiled, and that fadeth not away, reserved in heaven for you.

Now Peter focuses on the object of our confident hope. Reborn as members of God's family, we have a claim to "the family estate." But our inheritance with God is not the kind of thing that can fall apart or lose value as ordinary inheritances so often do. Rather, it is permanent: incapable of decay of any kind. That is because it is found in Heaven, in the presence of the eternal God (compare Matthew 6:20). It is, in fact, eternal life in God's presence, the very thing for which we were first made. That inheritance is now reserved for us, kept back for us to have on our arrival.

What Do You Think?

How does the inheritance we have in Christ contrast with worldly inheritances?

Talking Points for Your Discussion

- With regard to value
- With regard to how long they last
- With regard to how they may or may not be shared
- With regard to how they are obtained
- Other

Decay

Virtually everything on earth will decay. Food will rot. Clothing will mildew. Paper will decompose. Asphalt will disintegrate. Concrete will weather and crumble. Bones of dinosaurs can be dug up, but the mere existence of such bones testifies to the fact that the life they were once part of is no more.

Incorruptibility is not a characteristic of life on this earth. It doesn't happen in physical things, and it probably never happens in moral standards either. We see such standards decline as descriptions are cleverly reworded. For example, *prostitutes* are now called *sex workers* in some areas. This is merely a way to "call evil good" (Isaiah 5:20); it is a way to claim to be without sin (contrast 1 John 1:8). Such is the decay of the world.

Yet Peter promises that ultimately we will receive something incorruptible: an eternal inheritance reserved for us in Heaven. As Paul said, "This corruptible must put on incorruption, and this mortal must put on immortality" (1 Corinthians 15:53). A time is coming when all the decaying things of this world will be behind us. What a joy that will be! —J. B. N.

B. Protection (v. 5)

5. Who are kept by the power of God through faith unto salvation ready to be revealed in the last time.

As we anticipate receiving our inheritance, we can be confident not just that the inheritance is there but that we will indeed receive it. That confidence is not based on our own ability to "get through" to the end, however. It is founded on God's ability to see us through. God's power guards us through the hardships that we face as believers, allowing our faith to endure and even flourish when we might expect it to be quenched (compare 2 Corinthians 1:3-10; Revelation 3:10).

The outcome is the promised end-time salvation of God. To say that it will *be revealed in the last time* is not a frightening prospect for the Christian. God's end time indeed means the climax of His righteous judgment, but that is to be experienced by God's enemies. For those who are His family, the end means salvation, the final deliverance from all the problems and persecutions we face. It means God's victory, a victory that He shares with the entire family.

II. Believers Refined

(1 Peter 1:6-9)

A. Trials, Value, Result (vv. 6, 7)

6. Wherein ye greatly rejoice, though now for a season, if need be, ye are in heaviness through manifold temptations.

Eternal life in God's family is certainly something to rejoice about. But Peter makes clear that our rejoicing goes on even when the present is difficult. The Greek word behind the translation *temptations* is also translated "trial" in 1 Peter 4:12. Trials or persecutions can tempt believers to abandon the faith so that the persecution may stop. But those reading Peter's letter can face persecution because God's promise of final victory is sure.

That promise changes the believer's perspective on suffering in the present. The sufferings may be many and of all kinds. But compared with eternity, they are slight. So from the perspective of faith, they last *for a season,* just a short time.

Those sufferings are no accident; they do not happen because God's power has failed. Rather, they play a role in His plan. God does not cause them, but in His wisdom He uses them.

7. That the trial of your faith, being much more precious than of gold that perisheth, though it be tried with fire, might be found unto praise and honour and glory at the appearing of Jesus Christ.

The reasons for God allowing His people to suffer are many. No single explanation is sufficient, and much remains a mystery to us. But here Peter reminds readers of one outcome of our suffering under God's plan: faith that has endured suffering has been strengthened and proved genuine, like gold that has been refined and purified in a super-hot fire. If fire can refine earthly gold, which

HOW TO SAY IT

Asia	*Ay*-zha.
Bithynia	Bih-*thin*-ee-uh.
Cappadocia	Kap-uh-*doe*-shuh.
Galatia	Guh-*lay*-shuh.
Nostradamus	*Nahss*-truh-***dah***-mus.
Pontus	*Pon*-tuss.

passes away with this present age, then suffering can refine faith that endures forever and is immeasurably more valuable than gold (compare Isaiah 48:10; Zechariah 13:9; 1 Corinthians 3:13).

What Do You Think?

What difficulty has served as the most severe "trial of your faith" to this point? How have things turned out?

Talking Points for Your Discussion

- Challenges on the job to act in line with Christian ethics
- Cultural acceptance of immoral lifestyles
- Discrimination due to of faith conviction
- Other

B. Joy, Love, Goal (vv. 8, 9)

8. Whom having not seen, ye love; in whom, though now ye see him not, yet believing, ye rejoice with joy unspeakable and full of glory.

In the end, Jesus will be revealed to all as Lord; for now, He is unseen. But those with faith affirm His lordship even though we, like everyone else, cannot see Him. Therein lies the essence of faith: a confident belief and commitment in the unseen reality of the true God (John 20:29; 2 Corinthians 5:7; Hebrews 11:1).

That unseen reality enables us to rejoice even when what we do see is profoundly difficult. The suffering of the faithful is very real. But so is the power of the Lord, and so is the promise of His final victory. As a result, our rejoicing can continue at all times. It is *joy unspeakable* because it is based on the Lord who is beyond comparison with anything else. It is *full of glory* because it acknowledges Christ's unseen glory and anticipates the time when His glory will be revealed to all.

9. Receiving the end of your faith, even the salvation of your souls.

Again Peter reminds suffering Christians that their confident expectation of the future transforms their present. *The end* refers to a goal or intended outcome (compare Romans 6:22). The goal that God has for us is that we should be rescued from evil and so share in His victory. Troubles are real, but are insignificant compared with eternity.

III. Plan Fulfilled

(1 Peter 1:10-12)

A. Prophets Had Searched (vv. 10, 11)

10. Of which salvation the prophets have enquired and searched diligently, who prophesied of the grace that should come unto you.

Peter has put the present in perspective by comparing it with the future. Now he compares the future with the past, reminding believers that they are the objects of God's favor at the very climax of His historic plan of salvation.

The Old Testament prophets were God's inspired messengers, delivering His authoritative message to successive generations of Israelites. Their message both interpreted the present and promised the future that God would bring to reality. The present, according to those prophets, is characterized by rebellion against God. But God will prevail and accomplish His purpose, which is to turn the rebels into friends. That can come about only by God's grace—the favor and blessing He gives to those who do not deserve it.

The prophets had announced that one day God would accomplish that saving goal. But they did not live to see its coming. As faithful people, they longed to experience the climax of God's plan, or at least to know more about it (Matthew 13:17; Luke 10:24). Now believers in Christ are in the very position that the ancient prophets longed for!

Which Prophecies?

Belief in prophets, oracles, and seers was common in the paganism of the first century AD. Various "signs" were taken to indicate a person's future greatness. The problem is that these were recorded *after* the individual did in fact become great. Outside the Judeo-Christian heritage, there is virtually no evidence of valid predictive prophecy of a person's greatness before the person was born.

More recently, Nostradamus wrote a book of prophecies in the sixteenth century. Modern followers have claimed that he predicted world events centuries in advance. But a more objective view is that such claims are based on (sometimes deliberate) mistranslations or strained explanations of his original words.

Visual for Lesson 10. *Point to this visual as you introduce the discussion question that is associated with verse 16.*

By contrast, the Old Testament offers prophecies of influential leaders far in advance of their appearance (examples: Isaiah 45:1, 13; Daniel 8:9-11, 20, 21). The most important of these prophecies were those of Jesus and His ministry. Which prophets and prophecies do you trust? —J. B. N.

11. Searching what, or what manner of time the Spirit of Christ which was in them did signify, when it testified beforehand the sufferings of Christ, and the glory that should follow.

Through prophets, God repeatedly promised that He would deliver His people. The prophets knew the certainty of that promise, but they did not know exactly how God would fulfill it.

Writing from the perspective that knows how God fulfilled His promises, Peter discusses just how amazing God's plan is. The prophets delivered God's promise to His suffering people, and the prophets were themselves at the very center of the suffering (Matthew 5:12; 23:30, 35). In fulfilling the promise given through the prophets, God entered the world in the person of Jesus. He willingly accepted suffering and death. By that means Jesus overcame the sin and death that oppressed them. The prophets had revealed glimpses of this plan (Isaiah 53:1-12; Zechariah 13:7; etc.), but only as it is fulfilled do we see it clearly.

It was well established among believers in Israel's God that God's Spirit inspired the prophets to deliver their message. But here Peter refers to God's Spirit as *the Spirit of Christ.* This emphasizes not just that Jesus is the divine Son of God, but also that the Spirit of the Christ who suffered is the one who inspired the prophets who suffered. That in turn reminds the readers, who are experiencing suffering of their own, that the same Spirit lives in them. He enables them to fulfill God's plan in the midst of their difficulty.

To that reminder the readers can add the hope of future deliverance. Christ suffered, but then rose in glory. Presently Christ's people suffer, but at His return they will share in His glory. Since God has faithfully fulfilled His promise to send Christ, and since God faithfully raised Christ from the dead, then God will be faithful to send Christ again to bring the fullness of salvation to His people.

B. Answer Is Revealed (v. 12)

12. Unto whom it was revealed, that not unto themselves, but unto us they did minister the things, which are now reported unto you by them that have preached the gospel unto you with the Holy Ghost sent down from heaven; which things the angels desire to look into.

Believers in Christ stand at the focus of everything that God has done in history. We are the beneficiaries of the promises God made through the prophets. What the Holy Spirit promised through the prophets we have now received. Even the angels through the ages have longed to have a glimpse of what Christians now have.

The first readers of this letter may think of themselves as anything but privileged. But their position from God's perspective is quite different. They already have the blessings of the ages. That reminder provides them with a firm basis for the confident expectation that God will indeed deliver them fully when Christ returns.

IV. Holiness Required
(1 Peter 1:13-16)

A. Results Expected (vv. 13-15)

13. Wherefore gird up the loins of your mind, be sober, and hope to the end for the grace that is to be brought unto you at the revelation of Jesus Christ.

Peter now brings the issue of hope to the action step. To move quickly in biblical times, a man needs to pull up the hem of his robe and tie it around his waist with his cloth belt. This is what it means to *gird up the loins*—it signifies being ready for action (compare Luke 12:35).

For believers under persecution, the need is to have the mind fully instilled with the reality of the gospel. That perspective demands a specific attitude. It begins with soberness, or seriousness of mind. That does not imply humorlessness. Rather, it means that we have a sound, wise, and realistic assessment of the world around us. The sober person does not waste life on meaningless things. The gospel allows us to focus on God's purposes.

What Do You Think?

What specifically can you do to "gird up the loins of your mind" this week?

Talking Points for Your Discussion

- Regarding your knowledge of God's Word
- Regarding your prayer life
- Regarding your entertainment choices
- Other

14. As obedient children, not fashioning yourselves according to the former lusts in your ignorance.

Those who believe that their lives belong only to themselves imagine that they are free to do as they please. Those are the lusts of ignorance. But matters are different for those with a new birth into God's family. We want to please our Father. Saved in the past, with a hope for the future, our outlook in the present is entirely transformed.

15. But as he which hath called you is holy, so be ye holy in all manner of conversation.

To say that God is holy is to say that He is set apart and distinct—untouched by uncleanness. As members of His family, we are called to maintain the family resemblance. We live so that we are distinctly identified with God's character and purpose. The first-century readers are being persecuted because of their distinct lifestyle. Peter reminds them that they need to maintain that distinction despite its costs because of their vital identity as God's children. The word *conversation* in the *King James Version* here refers to all kinds of interaction with people, not just speech.

B. Reason Established (v. 16)

16. Because it is written, Be ye holy; for I am holy.

This quotation is found repeatedly in Leviticus (11:44, 45; 19:2; 20:7). That book emphasized to the Israelites how they were to live distinctively as God's people among the pagan nations. Because through the gospel Christians have the fulfillment of Israel's promises and confident expectation for the future, our obligation is all the greater to live in a way that shows our identity as God's people.

What Do You Think?

What do you most need to lay aside in your pursuit of holiness? How will you do it?

Talking Points for Your Discussion

- A material possession
- A secret sin
- A habit
- Other

Conclusion

A. Confident Expectation

A wag once said, "Christians are too heavenly minded to be any earthly good." That may be the most inaccurate assessment of Christianity ever given! Genuine hope, founded on the gospel, gives Christians the power to overcome all kinds of obstacles in the present as we live out God's plan and purpose in the world. A confident expectation of God's salvation does not make us passive and useless. It empowers us to live in a way that testifies to the Christ whose return we assuredly await.

B. Prayer

O God, You have done amazing things to make us part of Your family. Strengthen our hope for the future so that we can live as Your people in the present. In Jesus' name, amen.

C. Thought to Remember

"Those who have a 'why' to live can bear with almost any 'how.'" —Victor Frankl

INVOLVEMENT LEARNING

Some of the activities below are also found in the helpful student book, Adult Bible Class.
Don't forget to download the free reproducible page from www.standardlesson.com to enhance your lesson!

Into the Lesson

Have the following on the board as learners arrive: *Name things we accept or believe as true, even though we cannot or have not personally seen them.* Jot responses on the board. Possible responses among many are gravity, DNA molecules, carbon dioxide, germs, etc.

Ask, "Why do we accept these things as real?" After discussion, make the transition to Bible study by saying, "Peter reminds believers that we accept Jesus and His resurrection as true even without seeing Him. He calls this acceptance 'hope.' Hope should be a key word for every Christian's life."

Alternative: Place in chairs copies of the "Discovering the Key" activity from the reproducible page, which you can download. Learners can begin working on this exercise as they arrive.

Into the Word

Divide the class into five study teams of two to five each. (Larger classes may form additional teams to study duplicate topics; smaller classes can form fewer teams and double up some assignments.) Give each team a copy of the appropriate segment of the lesson commentary, a poster board, a marker, and the following instructions:

Hope Team: Clarify the intent of the word *hope* for today's study. Read the lesson's Introduction and Lesson Background for ideas. Illustrate how the word *hope* is used in 1 Peter 1:3.

Resurrection Team: Focusing on 1 Peter 1:3-5, clarify how Peter looks to the resurrection of Christ to bring hope to believers. Explain why verse 3 may be called *the key verse* for today's text. Explain how believers are "kept by the power of God through faith unto salvation" (v. 5).

Trials Team: Focusing on 1 Peter 1:6-9, clarify and illustrate Peter's teaching that hope is often refined in trials. Give a contemporary example of his gold illustration in verse 7.

Salvation Team: Focusing on 1 Peter 1:10-12, summarize and clarify how the past gives hope for our salvation, our future deliverance.

Action Team: Focusing on 1 Peter 1:13-16, list, explain, and illustrate how hope transforms the lives of believers.

Allow time for groups to share their conclusions.

Into Life

Say, "The word *hope* is a very common word in the Christian vocabulary. The *Hope Team* reminded us that Christians do not use that word in the way that it is used in many contemporary settings. We can illustrate the Christian idea of *hope* with songs." Ask each team to select a song that reflects any of the principles of hope taught in today's text. (*Option:* Distribute hymnals and/or other Christian songbooks for learners to consult for their selections.) Teams will share why they chose particular songs and tell how those songs demonstrate hope as taught in today's study.

Say, "Music is one way to share and teach hope to a new generation of believers. Why do you think it is important for each generation to learn this concept?" After some discussion, ask, "What are some other ways we can teach a new generation about this kind of hope?"

Distribute handouts with this heading: *My Last Will and Testament of Spiritual Things.* Include the following below the heading:

> *I, ___________, being spiritually minded, do wish to pass to my physical and/or spiritual children and grandchildren, this thought:* ______

Ask learners to write a sentence stating what spiritual heritage they would like to pass along. The statement should include the word *hope.*

Option: Distribute copies of the "Sharing Our Hope" activity from the reproducible page. Use this as a case study to discuss how the lesson text could be used to comfort a suffering Christian.

May 12
Lesson 11

SURE HOPE

DEVOTIONAL READING: Psalm 130
BACKGROUND SCRIPTURE: 2 Peter 1

2 PETER 1:2-15, 20, 21

2 Grace and peace be multiplied unto you through the knowledge of God, and of Jesus our Lord,

3 According as his divine power hath given unto us all things that pertain unto life and godliness, through the knowledge of him that hath called us to glory and virtue:

4 Whereby are given unto us exceeding great and precious promises: that by these ye might be partakers of the divine nature, having escaped the corruption that is in the world through lust.

5 And beside this, giving all diligence, add to your faith virtue; and to virtue knowledge;

6 And to knowledge temperance; and to temperance patience; and to patience godliness;

7 And to godliness brotherly kindness; and to brotherly kindness charity.

8 For if these things be in you, and abound, they make you that ye shall neither be barren nor unfruitful in the knowledge of our Lord Jesus Christ.

9 But he that lacketh these things is blind, and cannot see afar off, and hath forgotten that he was purged from his old sins.

10 Wherefore the rather, brethren, give diligence to make your calling and election sure: for if ye do these things, ye shall never fall:

11 For so an entrance shall be ministered unto you abundantly into the everlasting kingdom of our Lord and Saviour Jesus Christ.

12 Wherefore I will not be negligent to put you always in remembrance of these things, though ye know them, and be established in the present truth.

13 Yea, I think it meet, as long as I am in this tabernacle, to stir you up by putting you in remembrance;

14 Knowing that shortly I must put off this my tabernacle, even as our Lord Jesus Christ hath shewed me.

15 Moreover I will endeavour that ye may be able after my decease to have these things always in remembrance.

. . . .

20 Knowing this first, that no prophecy of the scripture is of any private interpretation.

21 For the prophecy came not in old time by the will of man: but holy men of God spake as they were moved by the Holy Ghost.

KEY VERSE

According as his divine power hath given unto us all things that pertain unto life and godliness, through the knowledge of him that hath called us to glory and virtue. —**2 Peter 1:3**

Undying Hope

Unit 3: A Call to Holy Living

Lessons 10–13

Lesson Aims

After participating in this lesson, each student will be able to:

1. List some of the gifts God has given us so that we have everything we need for a life of godliness.

2. Contrast Peter's concept of partaking of the divine nature with pagan concepts of "becoming gods."

3. Identify the quality of 2 Peter 1:5-7 where he or she is weakest and make a plan for change.

Lesson Outline

Introduction
- A. How Permanent Is "Permanent"?
- B. Lesson Background

I. Hope's Resources (2 Peter 1:2-4)
- A. Knowledge (vv. 2, 3)
- B. Promises (v. 4)

II. Hope's Character (2 Peter 1:5-9)
- A. Virtue Ladder (vv. 5-7)
  - *"Give Me a Drink!"*
- B. Fruitful Relationship (v. 8)
- C. Spiritual Sight (v. 9)

III. Hope's Persistence (2 Peter 1:10-15)
- A. In the Present (v. 10)
- B. For Eternity (v. 11)
  - *Everlasting*
- C. Until Death (vv. 12-15)

IV. Hope's Foundation (2 Peter 1:20, 21)
- A. What Is True (v. 20)
- B. Why It's True (v. 21)

Conclusion
- A. The Power of the Gospel
- B. Prayer
- C. Thought to Remember

Introduction

A. How Permanent Is "Permanent"?

As children we look forward to losing our temporary teeth and getting permanent ones. As adults we go to great effort to make those so-called permanent teeth last. We may go to the dentist for a temporary crown, to be replaced a week later with a permanent one. Then years later, that supposedly "permanent" work has to be repeated. Permanent did not turn out to mean "forever"!

It seldom does. A temporary worker has a job for a short period of time, but no job position is truly permanent. A temporary tattoo will wash right off, but even the permanent kind fades with time. Perhaps most difficult to make permanent is a change in one's life. Most humans know that they need a better kind of life. But finding a way to make the right change and make it permanent is difficult. Today's text is about making change that is permanent for this life and beyond.

B. Lesson Background

In many respects, 2 Peter is the sequel to 1 Peter (see the background to last week's lesson). The focus of 2 Peter is on that apostle's final instructions as he anticipates his pending death. We might say that this letter is Peter's "last will and testament." As such, it is a discourse on what he realizes the rising generation of Christians needs, the lessons he has learned through a lifetime of following Jesus in a sinful world.

The letter focuses on a few key topics, including the life that results from the genuine message of God (2 Peter 1), resistance to false and immoral teachers (2 Peter 2), and patience and expectancy regarding Christ's return (2 Peter 3). This week's text belongs to that first section. We think 2 Peter was written in AD 67 or 68.

I. Hope's Resources

(2 Peter 1:2-4)

A. Knowledge (vv. 2, 3)

2. Grace and peace be multiplied unto you through the knowledge of God, and of Jesus our Lord.

This letter begins with the kind of greeting that we find in most New Testament letters. Having identified himself and addressed the readers in verse 1, Peter now offers a salutation that is significant for what he is about to say. In the Greek language of the New Testament, the word for *grace* sounds much like another word commonly used as a greeting. Christians play on that similarity, turning their word of greeting into a reminder of God's undeserved favor. *Peace* is the standard greeting among Jewish people. It is used by Christians, both Jews and non-Jews, to affirm that God's long-anticipated peace is now delivered by Christ.

Peter here does not simply proclaim that these gifts are available, but prays that they may grow for the readers. Because the readers of this letter have true knowledge of God, not some myth or human creation, they are on a path that must yield an ever-increasing change in their lives.

3. According as his divine power hath given unto us all things that pertain unto life and godliness, through the knowledge of him that hath called us to glory and virtue.

The gifts in Christ provide the sure foundation for the life that God intends for us. Four key words, appearing in two pairs, express this. The first word in each pair describes a gift from God, and the second describes our response.

The first pair is *life and godliness.* The word *life* is a reminder that real life is available only as God's gift in Christ. *Godliness* refers to a style of life that properly honors God in obedience.

The second pair is *glory and virtue.* The preposition *to* in front of this pair is a little tricky because there is no preposition in the Greek text; it has to be supplied by the translator for smooth reading. Perhaps your copy of the *King James Version* has a footnote that offers *by* as a possible alternative. In either case, we look forward to the time when God's glorious nature will be revealed fully. We share His glory because He promises to share His victory with the people who belong to Him by His grace.

Virtue, the second half of this pair, may sound like an old-fashioned word to us. In its biblical context it refers to an excellent style of life, one that reflects the real purpose for which we exist.

What Do You Think?

In which areas that deal with living a life of godliness have you grown the most in the past year? Why?

Talking Points for Your Discussion

- With regard to your prayer life
- With regard to your worship
- With regard to your Christian service
- With regard to your Bible knowledge
- Other

B. Promises (v. 4)

4. Whereby are given unto us exceeding great and precious promises: that by these ye might be partakers of the divine nature, having escaped the corruption that is in the world through lust.

Again, Peter emphasizes the way that God has given gifts that motivate lasting and growing change. The *exceeding great and precious promises* are the ones now fulfilled in Christ, though also awaiting ultimate fulfillment at Christ's return.

The result is that we belong to God. To be *partakers of the divine nature* means not that we become part of God, as if we are somehow absorbed into His being. Rather, it means that we share identity with Him as members of His family. The blessing of union with Christ gives us resurrection life and power but also unites us with Him in suffering in a sinful world (1 Peter 4:13; 5:1).

By contrast, the people who belong to the world share an existence characterized by corruption, the decay that comes from death. Such a life is driven by out-of-control desires *(lust).*

What Do You Think?

What helps you most to resist falling back into worldly corruption? How so?

Talking Points for Your Discussion

- An accountability partner
- Support of fellow believers
- Personal Bible study
- Prayer
- Other

II. Hope's Character

(2 PETER 1:5-9)

A. Virtue Ladder (vv. 5-7)

5a. And beside this, giving all diligence, add to your faith virtue.

Having reflected on how the gifts of the gospel provide the basis for lasting and growing change, Peter now details the nature of that change. He does this with a ladder of virtues, a step-by-step description of the characteristics that build on one another as a person grows in Christian hope. The steps of this ladder are of supreme importance. Therefore, this process demands that we give *all diligence* in displaying a consistent energy and enthusiasm befitting these most valuable pursuits.

The foundational virtue is *faith.* Faith, of course, is the response of belief and trust that we give God as He reaches out to us with the gospel.

The first step up from faith is *virtue.* We can refer to the entire ladder as listing virtues, but here the word is used more specifically to mean "excellent behavior" (see also v. 3, above). Faith is always to produce behavioral change. What kind of person truly believes something yet does nothing about it? Lasting change founded on Christ depends on these first two steps.

5b. And to virtue knowledge.

The antidote to false ideas is true *knowledge,* founded on what God has done and revealed in history, climaxing in Jesus. Just as initial faith must lead to behavioral change, it must also lead to a thirst to know more fully the good news that prompts our faith.

6a. And to knowledge temperance.

Older uses of the word *temperance* may lead us to think in terms of "sobriety" (avoidance of alcoholic beverages). But the idea is broader than that—along the lines of "self-restraint." Without God in the picture, a person has no clear reason to restrain desires and impulses as they arise. Through Christ we receive both the reason and the power to put our desires under control.

"GIVE ME A DRINK!"

Some years ago, a friend of mine was telling me of his years as an Air Force chaplain. At one assignment he met a young man struggling with alcohol. The man's marriage was about to come apart, and he was in danger of being dishonorably discharged for unreliability.

Through discussion, Bible study, and a good deal of prayer, the young man accepted Christ as Lord and found the power to overcome his addiction. His marriage revived, and he became a respected individual.

Then one day he wandered into the club on base where alcoholic drinks were available. The bartender, aware of the young man's previous condition, urged him not to drink. The young man insisted. As the bartender continued to refuse, the young man raised his voice.

Finally, the bartender relented and asked him what he wanted to drink. "Seven-Up," the young man replied. With a smile, the bartender served him. The young man took his drink, turned to the crowd that was staring at him, raised his glass in a toast, drank it down, and walked out. The power of the gospel had helped him regain the virtue of self-restraint. It can do so for us as well.—J. B. N.

6b. And to temperance patience.

Patience especially signifies endurance in hardship. When we belong to Christ, we have a powerful impulse toward such endurance in the assurance of salvation already granted and the hope of salvation's fullness yet to be received. We can face the troubles of the present knowing that God is faithful.

6c. And to patience godliness.

Godliness has already been mentioned in verse 3. In Peter's time, most people believe in showing proper respect to the gods. But which god or gods are true? Knowing the true God is the foundation of genuine godliness, and the gospel teaches us to know Him as both righteous and merciful. So true godliness pursues righteousness and mercy in respectful imitation of God himself. To do otherwise is to deny the faith on which all the virtues are founded.

7a. And to godliness brotherly kindness.

As godliness looks up to God, brotherly kindness looks around to others. God's love compels us to love others. Such regard is expressed in tangible deeds (1 John 3:17). This is the characteristic that people should see among us as we live according to our identity as the people of God.

7b. And to brotherly kindness charity.

God loves the unlovable, the sinner. So the Christian's love does not stop at the church door. To brotherly kindness we are compelled to add the gracious, unconditional love—here called *charity*—that God has shown to us. These two steps of the virtue ladder should speak to the intensity and universality of God's love as practiced by His people.

We should note well the overall scope of the ladder of virtues. It begins with *faith,* the foundational characteristic. It ends with the exercise of *love,* the deep expression of God's relationship with us. The ladder is grounded throughout on *hope,* the confident expectation of God's saving actions yet to come. The three great keystones of the Christian life—faith, love, and hope—are very much on display here (compare 1 Corinthians 13:13).

B. Fruitful Relationship (v. 8)

8. For if these things be in you, and abound, they make you that ye shall neither be barren nor unfruitful in the knowledge of our Lord Jesus Christ.

Unfruitfulness is a grave danger! The Scriptures repeatedly use images of plants that do not bear fruit to remind God's people how serious is their response to God (examples: Isaiah 5:1-7; Luke 13:6-9; John 15:1-8). What Peter describes is the necessary, vital fruit of a relationship with Christ. These fruits need to *abound,* growing more abundant as time passes to reflect the magnitude of what God has done for us.

What Do You Think?

How do you recognize when unfruitfulness is starting to manifest itself in your life?

Talking Points for Your Discussion

- Matthew 13:22
- Luke 19:20-23
- John 15:2-6
- Ephesians 4:29-31; 5:3, 4
- 2 Timothy 4:10
- Other

Visual for Lesson 11. *Point to this visual as you explore the connection between a good personal harvest and making one's calling sure.*

C. Spiritual Sight (v. 9)

9. But he that lacketh these things is blind, and cannot see afar off, and hath forgotten that he was purged from his old sins.

To claim faith and then not live as Peter has described reflects spiritual blindness, or at least something like nearsightedness—the inability to see beyond our own noses to the truth of what God has done and how we need to respond. If we remember that God has cleansed us from the rebellion that was our old life, then we will want nothing more than for the new life to take root and bear fruit in every way.

III. Hope's Persistence

(2 Peter 1:10-15)

A. In the Present (v. 10)

10. Wherefore the rather, brethren, give diligence to make your calling and election sure: for if ye do these things, ye shall never fall.

With a confident expectation of the future, we can persist in the present. Peter insists on this, reminding us that we do not want to lose out on what belongs to us by God's grace.

This calls for *diligence,* the same kind of characteristic named in verse 5. What is at stake is our *calling and election.* These two terms remind us of ancient Israel's identity as God's people, called His "chosen" or "elect" (Isaiah 42:1; 45:4; etc.). By His saving death and resurrection, Christ has made His followers the called and elect.

To keep that identity, Christ's followers need to maintain connection with Him. If we abandon the faith, we lose our standing as His people (compare Hebrews 2:1; 6:11; 10:35, 36). We should note carefully what Peter says here. He is not discussing the ongoing struggle with sin that every believer experiences. Rather, he warns that if we ignore the mandate to grow in virtue then we can lose the gift that we have received by faith. That is what it means to *fall.* A growing faith is a secure faith.

B. For Eternity (v. 11)

11. For so an entrance shall be ministered unto you abundantly into the everlasting kingdom of our Lord and Saviour Jesus Christ.

With our eyes clearly on the object of our hope, we have every reason to persist in the present. What God has for His called and chosen people is citizenship under His king, Jesus, who will rule without end in justice and peace. This is the gift He has prepared for us in the future, even as we are experiencing Christ's rule now through our growing faith. That future connects with our present, reminding us how important are the changes that God is working in our lives.

Everlasting

The related words *eternal, everlasting,* and *forever* are often used in a loose sense. I once saw a commercial for a cemetery that offered "eternal care" for grave sites. I doubt that the cemetery will last that long. When our family was younger and we were taking a long car trip, the children would often complain, "It's taking forever!" Not quite, but it seemed a very long time to them.

There is a very interesting usage of the word *forever* in Roman Catholic history. In the eighteenth century, the Jesuits had become a significant force within the church. Individual Jesuits were very active in the governments of several Catholic countries. Many folk in those countries came to fear the organized power of the Jesuits and demanded their elimination. The Jesuits were banished from country after country, and ultimately Pope Clement XIV banned the order "forever" in 1773. In the next century, however, the political situation changed drastically, and Pope Pius VII restored the Jesuit order in 1814. Apparently, *forever* meant 41 years!

In spite of the fact that earthly conditions can and do change, we can be assured that the *everlasting* kingdom of Jesus really is *forever.* —J. B. N.

C. Until Death (vv. 12-15)

12. Wherefore I will not be negligent to put you always in remembrance of these things, though ye know them, and be established in the present truth.

Peter's life is about to reach its end (v. 14, below), but he is determined to use the time he has left to reinforce God's saving message. *These things* of which he writes are well-known among his readers, but they are so important that they bear repeating. Peter does not stress them because he questions his readers' standing with God, but because this is the most important message he can share.

13, 14. Yea, I think it meet, as long as I am in this tabernacle, to stir you up by putting you in remembrance; knowing that shortly I must put off this my tabernacle, even as our Lord Jesus Christ hath shewed me.

Peter uses the word *tabernacle,* or tent (Exodus 40:2), to indicate his physical body (compare 2 Corinthians 5:1). He chooses this image to stress the shortness of his life. As the end of life approaches, we expect people to do what matters most to them. Because time is short, it is precious and must be used for what is most valuable. Peter, at the end of his life, stresses that what matters most to him is encouraging believers by reminding them of what they have received.

We wonder how the Lord Jesus showed Peter that his death was near (compare John 21:18, 19). Though we cannot answer that question, we can observe Peter's confidence in knowing that Christ will deliver him into His presence.

HOW TO SAY IT

Corinthians	Ko-*rin*-thee-unz (*th* as in *thin*).
Isaiah	Eye-*zay*-uh.
tabernacle	***tah***-burr-*nah*-kul.

15. Moreover I will endeavour that ye may be able after my decease to have these things always in remembrance.

Peter wants to ensure that Christians will have access to this valuable message after he departs, so he writes it in a letter. The letter should not end up on a dusty shelf. Its message is not only to be preserved, but copied and circulated.

What Do You Think?

What words of spiritual encouragement would you like to pass on to others before you die? What's keeping you from doing this now?

Talking Points for Your Discussion

- To a child or grandchild (2 Timothy 1:5)
- To a child "in the faith" (1 Timothy 1:2)
- To a close friend in Christ
- To an unbeliever
- Other

IV. Hope's Foundation

(2 Peter 1:20, 21)

A. What Is True (v. 20)

20. Knowing this first, that no prophecy of the scripture is of any private interpretation.

In verses 16-19 (not in today's text), Peter reminds his readers that he is an eyewitness to the ministry of Jesus. Coupled with the assurance of such testimony is the message of Israel's Scriptures, what we call the Old Testament.

Because all the books of Scripture are the products of God's inspiration, they can all be referred to as *prophecy*. In this regard, *prophecy* means not just prediction of the future, but also the announcement of God's message. The sacred writings are not the product of human imagination. *Private interpretation* does not refer to an individual's own reading and explanation of the Scriptures, but to their being written in the first place. The Scriptures exist because God himself has provided them. The next verse makes this clearer.

B. Why It's True (v. 21)

21. For the prophecy came not in old time by the will of man: but holy men of God spake as they were moved by the Holy Ghost.

Peter reminds us that the witness of the Old Testament is the consequence of God's actions through His Holy Spirit. This is what Christians call *the doctrine of inspiration:* that the Holy Spirit worked through the writers of Scripture to produce the genuine Word of God (2 Timothy 3:16). It is true in all that it affirms, focused on the precise message that God wants delivered.

Our hope is founded on this divinely inspired message that points to the one of whom Peter was a witness: Jesus Christ. We have every reason to be confident in the truth of Jesus' message, in the certainty of what He has done to save us.

What Do You Think?

How should we respond to a fellow believer who expresses doubts about the inspiration and infallibility of Scripture?

Talking Points for Your Discussion

- In attitude
- In teaching
- In fellowship
- Deciding how he or she may or may not be used in the church's various ministries
- Other

Conclusion

A. The Power of the Gospel

The truth of the gospel is a powerful force. When we discover it, it inspires a confident expectation of the future that transforms our present lives. It inspires us to pursue the virtues that spring from the gospel and to grow in them consistently and constantly. No wonder Peter was compelled to share again that message in his last days on earth! The question is, what will we do with the message that he shared?

B. Prayer

Father, we are overwhelmed at what You have done! We look back and find reassurance. We look forward and have hope. Empower us to grow in our devotion to You. In Jesus' name, amen.

C. Thought to Remember

Make Peter's focus your own.

Involvement Learning

Some of the activities below are also found in the helpful student book, Adult Bible Class.
Don't forget to download the free reproducible page from www.standardlesson.com to enhance your lesson!

Into the Lesson

Apply a temporary tattoo on your hand as the class watches. Say, "These things are temporary, they will wash off quickly. Permanent tattoos, however, are much more durable. What are some other illustrations of 'temporary' versus 'permanent'?" Jot answers on the board.

Ask, "Are the things we have listed as 'permanent' really permanent? Why, or why not?" The lesson Introduction will give ideas why nothing in this world is really permanent, including tattoos. Say, "Today's study is about making a life change that is permanent in an eternal sense."

Into the Word

Read the printed text aloud, and then distribute a handout featuring two activities. The first activity will have the heading *Gifts and Responses, 2 Peter 1:3, 4.* Under it have three short columns, headed "Gifts," "Our Response," and "Interpretation or Application." Under the first column, list the word *life.* Say, "Peter wishes to help believers be effective and fruitful. In that light, he assures us of the gifts God has given and our appropriate responses. One gift is already listed for you. List one more gift and two responses cited in verse 3. You don't need to address the third column yet." Call for discoveries. *(Answers under "Gifts": life, glory; under "Our Response": godliness, virtue.)* Discuss per the lesson commentary.

Call learners' attention to the third column as you pose these questions: 1. How and why is *godliness* an appropriate response to the gift of life in Christ? 2. How and why is *virtue* (an excellent lifestyle) an appropriate response now to the glory we will share in Christ?" Consult the lesson commentary to clarify responses. Conclude the activity by saying, "Verse 4 reminds us that God has given promises that motivate growing change. Peter builds on this as he sketches what might be called 'a ladder of virtues.'"

The second activity on the handout, headed *Ladder of Virtues, 2 Peter 1:5-9,* will include the image of a ladder with eight rungs. Say, "In verses 5-9, Peter uses what might be called *a ladder of virtues* to discuss the nature of growth that should be evident in our lives. These characteristics build on one another as we grow in Christian hope."

Ask learners to scan the verses and write the characteristics on the ladder in ascending order. The characteristics, in order, are: *faith, virtue, knowledge, temperance, patience, godliness, brotherly kindness,* and *charity.* Ask for definitions or examples of each rung or step of Peter's ladder of virtues. Be sure to discuss the different senses of the word *virtue* as that word is used to describe both the ladder as a whole and as a specific rung on the ladder.

Option 1: To reinforce this segment of the lesson, distribute copies of the "Discovering a Sure Hope" activity from the reproducible page, which you can download. Say, "Please close your Bibles and see if you can complete this from what you have learned so far." Have learners score their own results.

Option 2: For a contrast with the "Ladder of Virtues" activity above, distribute copies of the "Bad Ladder" activity from the reproducible page. Have learners complete it as indicated.

Into Life

Say, "A *collage* is a collection of pictures of related scenes. We will attempt to create a 'verbal collage' from the eight rungs of our 'ladder of virtue.'" Scatter around the board the eight words of the ladder of virtues. Ask the class for word pictures to represent the eight words on the board. The resulting verbal pictures should illustrate how to live out the characteristics. For example, the verbal picture "someone reading the Bible" could be placed next to *knowledge.* Discuss how to personalize these depictions.

Active Hope

Devotional Reading: Luke 16:10-13
Background Scripture: 1 Peter 4

1 Peter 4:1-11

1 Forasmuch then as Christ hath suffered for
us in the flesh, arm yourselves likewise with
the same mind: for he that hath suffered in the
flesh hath ceased from sin;
2 That he no longer should live the rest of
his time in the flesh to the lusts of men, but to
the will of God.
3 For the time past of our life may suffice us
to have wrought the will of the Gentiles, when
we walked in lasciviousness, lusts, excess of
wine, revellings, banquetings, and abomina-
ble idolatries:

4 Wherein they think it strange that ye run
not with them to the same excess of riot, speak-
ing evil of you:
5 Who shall give account to him that is
ready to judge the quick and the dead.
6 For for this cause was the gospel preached
also to them that are dead, that they might be
judged according to men in the flesh, but live
according to God in the spirit.
7 But the end of all things is at hand: be ye
therefore sober, and watch unto prayer.
8 And above all things have fervent charity
among yourselves: for charity shall cover the
multitude of sins.
9 Use hospitality one to another without
grudging.
10 As every man hath received the gift, even
so minister the same one to another, as good
stewards of the manifold grace of God.
11 If any man speak, let him speak as the
oracles of God; if any man minister, let him do
it as of the ability which God giveth: that God
in all things may be glorified through Jesus
Christ, to whom be praise and dominion for
ever and ever. Amen.

Key Verse

As every man hath received the gift, even so minister the same one to another, as good stewards of the manifold grace of God. —**1 Peter 4:10**

Photo: Jupiterimages / Comstock / Thinkstock

Undying Hope

Unit 3: A Call to Holy Living

Lessons 10–13

Lesson Aims

After participating in this lesson, each student will be able to:

1. Describe key differences between the old, worldly life and new life in Christ.
2. Explain why and how Christ's physical suffering bears on the believer's behavior today.
3. Identify one gift God has given him or her and describe how he or she is using it—or will use it—as a steward of God's grace.

Lesson Outline

Introduction
- A. Wearing the Team Colors
- B. Lesson Background

I. Distinctive Life (1 Peter 4:1-6)
- A. Dead to Sin (vv. 1, 2)
- B. Different from Pagans (vv. 3-6)
  - *Undo*

II. Expectant Life (1 Peter 4:7-11)
- A. Alert and Praying (v. 7)
- B. Loving (v. 8)
- C. Hospitable (v. 9)
  - *The Practice of Hospitality*
- D. Serving (vv. 10, 11)

Conclusion
- A. Past, Present, and Future
- B. Prayer
- C. Thought to Remember

Introduction

A. Wearing the Team Colors

Perhaps you have noticed that people like to wear clothing that bears the colors and logos of their favorite sports teams. People dress this way to make their loyalties clear.

How do followers of Jesus display their "team colors"? Some Christians wear distinctive clothing, and one can buy T-shirts and caps emblazoned with Christian slogans. But we recognize that something other than clothing is what declares a person to be a follower of Jesus.

That "something different" is a way of life. Our lifestyle reflects what Christ has already done, what Christ will do in the future, and who we are as a result. It has to do with how we think, how we speak, and how we act. Without exception, the new way of life is what the New Testament provides as the distinguishing mark of the Christian. That subject is the focus of today's text.

B. Lesson Background

Today's text takes us back to 1 Peter to address the situation faced by its original readers. They were subjects of the Roman Empire, living in places and a time when the Romans were increasingly hostile to Christianity. With some localized exceptions (such as in Acts 18:2), Roman hostility did not extend to Jews as such. Roman respect for Judaism is traced to decisions and actions of Emperor Julius Caesar, who died in 44 BC.

Roman suspicion of Christians grew as the Romans began to realize that Christianity was a new faith, not just a subset of Judaism. The result was increasing persecution of Christians (see the Lesson Background to Lesson 10). This is probably why Peter refers to Rome by the code word "Babylon" in 1 Peter 5:13.

Identity was important to these Christians. It was their identity that had created the trouble they were experiencing. Could they maintain that identity, expressing it consistently in the face of pressure to abandon it? Their challenge was to be true to their Lord. Their lives were to reflect what He had done and promised to do, not simply enduring the pressure that they faced.

I. Distinctive Life

(1 Peter 4:1-6)

A. Dead to Sin (vv. 1, 2)

1. Forasmuch then as Christ hath suffered for us in the flesh, arm yourselves likewise with the same mind: for he that hath suffered in the flesh hath ceased from sin.

Peter begins by reminding his readers how their life with Christ began. It is first of all Christ's death that makes them His. By dying on the cross, He took the penalty for the sins of the world. Rising from the dead, He overcame and defeated sin. His death and resurrection therefore mean, in a very real and important sense, that sin is over. Its rule is finished.

Christians are united with Jesus in His resurrection and its victory over sin (Romans 6:3-6). The resurrection life is, ideally, a life free from sin. That does not mean that sinful behaviors and temptations suddenly disappear. Sin and Satan remain active in this present age, though they are genuinely defeated. Those united with Christ in His death and resurrection have to fight deliberately against sin with the consciousness of a new life and the strength that Christ provides.

So Peter uses a military expression, *arm yourselves,* and focuses on our foundational issue of intent, *with the same mind.* We must believe and insist that we are dead to sin so that we can live the resurrection life to keep sin in its defeated state. Since we have eternal life, we ought to pursue sin's defeat now, not just wait for its full and final elimination in eternity.

What Do You Think?

What attitudes and practices of Jesus do you most need to develop as you "arm" yourself for the Christian life?

Talking Points for Your Discussion

- Jesus' method and practice of prayer (Luke 5:16)
- Jesus' choice of companions (Luke 7:34)
- Jesus' sense of priorities (John 4:31-34)
- Jesus' self-denial (John 6:38)
- Other

2. That he no longer should live the rest of his time in the flesh to the lusts of men, but to the will of God.

Our transformation in Christ is to produce the identifying signs of new life in Him. In the old life, there is nothing to drive a person except one's own desires (*the lusts of men* refers to all kinds of desires, not just sexual desires). In Christ our motivation is changed: doing God's will is now paramount.

The good news of Jesus shows us how miserable our lives were when we pursued our own desires. The good news shows us how much God has done for us, driving us to replace a focus on our own desires with a focus on God's will.

B. Different from Pagans (vv. 3-6)

3. For the time past of our life may suffice us to have wrought the will of the Gentiles, when we walked in lasciviousness, lusts, excess of wine, revellings, banquetings, and abominable idolatries.

The persecuted Christians who read this letter live in a world dominated by pagan religions. These offer little or no moral teaching, and some even encourage indulgence in sex and alcohol. The lives of pagans, or *Gentiles* in this verse, reflect the excesses of human desires without boundaries.

So Peter reminds his readers of the kinds of self-destructive behaviors still around them, behaviors they used to practice themselves. *Lasciviousness* is unrestricted sexual activity. *Lusts* also suggests strong sexual desire, underlining the excesses of the old life. *Excess of wine* is drunkenness, of course. *Revellings* and *banquetings* add additional underlines that refer to gatherings for overindulgence in food, intoxicating drink, and immoral activity.

The list reaches its high point (or low point!) with *abominable idolatries.* This is the worship of false gods, a practice that lies at the heart of all the others. It often accompanies the most obvious displays of self-indulgence. Idols may be broadly described as gods made to fulfill human desires, gods made in human image. It is little wonder, then, that idolatry is listed alongside the things described here—human desires gone out of control. In worshipping idols, people in effect worship their own desires (compare Philippians 3:19).

Undo

When I replaced my old computer years ago, I discovered to my enjoyment that the new computer came equipped with a few games. I told myself that I could play a game or two while between projects because it was a bit of a break that kept my mind fresh. My favorite games became Free Cell and Spider Solitaire. I usually won at both, but occasionally I would work myself into a hole and lose. This happened in spite of the fact that both games had an "undo" feature that allowed me to reverse the last move. But reversing just the last move often wasn't enough; I still lost.

Then a couple of years ago I bought a laptop. The Free Cell and Spider Solitaire games that came with it also had an "undo" feature, but this one was different. It wasn't limited to just the last move; I could "undo" all the way back to the beginning if necessary. Since then I haven't lost a game!

I have often wondered, *Wouldn't life be more satisfying if it came with an "undo" feature?* Yet the sacrifice of Christ on the cross is exactly that! It undoes all the sin we have committed and gives us a clean slate with God. With this great "undo" available, why would we ever want to "redo" our sinful moves and go back to our old, eternally losing behavior? —J. B. N.

4. Wherein they think it strange that ye run not with them to the same excess of riot, speaking evil of you.

The behaviors of verse 3 used to be the norm for the readers of Peter's letter. But now such behaviors are part of the past. This fact is a source of tension between Peter's audience and their pagan neighbors. The harsh words of pagans against the restrained Christian lifestyle undoubtedly hurts. That very fact demonstrates the enormous change that has come to the Christians' lives.

5. Who shall give account to him that is ready to judge the quick and the dead.

Though the pagans ridicule the Christians' new behavior, they have reason to consider the matter soberly. In the end, all people—both *the quick* (living) and *the dead*—will stand before the true, righteous God who judges all His creation (also Acts 10:42; 2 Timothy 4:1). The difference between the pagans and the Christians will tell the story of judgment. One group rejects God and worships its own desires. The other turns to God for His mercy. The marks of identity are clear for each.

The idea of God's coming judgment is not pleasant to contemplate, but humans universally long for justice to prevail. If in the end there is no judgment from God, then there is no justice in the world. But if God does judge and I am guilty, what can I do? That realization drives us to accept God's offer of mercy.

> *What Do You Think?*
>
> What is your attitude when thinking of the judgment that unbelievers face? What changes do you need to make in this regard?
>
> *Talking Points for Your Discussion*
>
> - Satisfaction—they will get what they deserve
> - Thankfulness—"I was lost, but now I'm found"
> - Guilt—for ever sharing their lifestyle
> - Helplessness—just knowing their fate
> - Compassion—how can I reach them?
> - Other

6. For for this cause was the gospel preached also to them that are dead, that they might be judged according to men in the flesh, but live according to God in the spirit.

This verse is difficult to understand. However, with care for the setting of the letter, we probably can make good sense of Peter's meaning. The phrase *them that are dead* seems to refer to Christian victims of persecution. The gospel had been preached to them, and they believed it before dying. Therefore, even though humans have judged them harshly by worldly standards, with God those deceased believers enjoy life everlasting. They are the recipients of life everlasting through God's mercy that they had received while alive.

The outcome for the faithful stands in stark contrast with that of the pagans. In the final judgment, the latter will find themselves without hope, having rejected God's offer of mercy in the gospel. When we as Christians assess our own place in the world, we need to remember that the human view and God's view are very different. By the human view, the persecuted Christians were judged as wrongdoers. From God's perspective, it will be their persecutors who deserve judgment.

God's purpose in announcing the coming judgment is to enable sinful people to escape His wrath. The announcement of judgment is an act of God's mercy. How ironic it is, then, if people reject the warning because they find it harsh!

II. Expectant Life

(1 Peter 4:7-11)

A. Alert and Praying (v. 7)

7. But the end of all things is at hand: be ye therefore sober, and watch unto prayer.

The end or goal for which God has prepared the world *is at hand,* Peter reminds his readers (compare Romans 13:11, 12; 1 John 2:18). His previous discussion of God's judgment raises this topic to the forefront. But to our minds, the question we ask ourselves is how *the end of all things* could truly have been *at hand* in the first century since nearly 2,000 years now have passed and Christ still has not returned. To understand Peter's statement, we need to think carefully about what the New Testament teaches about the nearness of the end in comparison with the uncertainty of its timing.

Jesus affirmed both that His return was "near" (Matthew 24:33, 34) and that no one could know the time in advance (24:36). In light of both statements, we can understand that the nearness of His return is not calculated by a specific measure of time. Rather, the nearness of Jesus' return is a word of personal assurance to all His people: Jesus returns soon enough to rescue every one of His people from the sinful world and bring them together into the fullness of His kingdom.

With that assurance, coupled with the knowledge that the time is uncertain, we realize that we need to live expectantly and urgently. We anticipate Christ's return, and so we live with confidence while valuing every moment as an opportunity for serving Christ.

That is the message of this verse—that believers be *sober,* meaning "serious-minded." We are to be like sentries on the watch, always alert. But our alertness is directed to prayer, calling on God for assistance and relying on Him to guide and sustain us in these last days. Recognizing that our time on earth is short, we prayerfully grasp the urgency of the moment: to do God's will now.

What Do You Think?

How does (and should) the nearness of the end affect your daily service for Christ?

Talking Points for Your Discussion

- Matthew 24:36-48
- 1 Corinthians 7:29-31
- 1 John 2:18, 24-28
- Revelation 1:3
- Other

B. Loving (v. 8)

8. And above all things have fervent charity among yourselves: for charity shall cover the multitude of sins.

Our identity with Christ is based on the self-sacrificial, unconditional love of God that sent His Son into the world. As a result, nothing is more important in the life of the Christian than expressing that same self-sacrificial, unconditional love (here translated as *charity*) for others. So Peter says that living love—love that is *fervent* or especially strong—is the supreme pursuit of the Christian who lives in hope of Christ's return.

The expression *charity shall cover the multitude of sins* is a quotation of Proverbs 10:12. It is also found in James 5:20, and through repetition it has passed into our language as a cliché. Because the phrase is so familiar, we need to pay careful attention to get its meaning. In Proverbs and so here, it can mean that because of love, we should willingly forgive and forget the sins of others. When we do, we effectively hide their sins with loving forgiveness. Or Peter could be reminding us that

HOW TO SAY IT

Caesar	*See*-zer.
Gentiles	*Jen*-tiles.
lasciviousness	luh-*sih*-vee-us-nuss.
Lucian	*Loo*-shun.
Samosata	Suh-*mah*-suh-tah.

God's love, the love that sent Christ, hides our sin as Christ removes it. Or He could be suggesting that by living in love, we will avoid sinning against others, hiding sin by eliminating it.

In all these cases, the supreme importance of love is stressed. The reminder is to respond to God's love with active, sincere love for others in all situations. For believers facing persecution, this is a special reminder not to retaliate against the persecutors. Instead, we respond to evil with good, showing love even to enemies (Luke 6:27, 35).

C. Hospitable (v. 9)

9. Use hospitality one to another without grudging.

One practical expression of love is to share one's home and food. The practice of hospitality is vital to the first-century church. It is a means of providing for people in material need, for furthering the work of traveling evangelists, and for nurturing the fellowship of the church (Romans 16:23; 3 John 8). Hospitality is particularly important in times of persecution, as Christians meet the needs of their suffering brothers and sisters by welcoming them into their homes.

Lucian of Samosata, who lived in the second century AD, wrote humorously about Christians overwhelming their imprisoned brothers and sisters with gifts of food and clothing while standing outside their cells singing hymns to God hour after hour. It is impressive when a humorist can find nothing to ridicule about Christians except their great devotion to hospitality!

Visual for Lesson 12. *As you consider verses 10 and 11, point to this visual and ask, "What ministry opportunities will you seek out in the week ahead?"*

What Do You Think?

What are some specific ways that you can better extend hospitality?

Talking Points for Your Discussion

- Toward the needy (Matthew 25:35)
- Toward enemies (Romans 12:20)
- Toward strangers (Hebrews 13:2)
- Toward fellow Christians (3 John 5-8)

But such practical expressions of love can be a costly chore. So Peter reminds believers to practice hospitality *without grudging*—without the kind of muttering grumbles that characterizes a person who is irritated or angry. Real love is generous, and real generosity is free of resentment. We are to remember that our hospitality is an expression of love in response to God's love for us.

The Practice of Hospitality

I have heard of, read about, and experienced numerous instances of people living in impoverished countries who provided extraordinary hospitality to visitors. Those providing the hospitality may have very little compared with American standards, but they have been known to offer abundant food and even housing to Western visitors nonetheless.

When national church conventions were held in the nineteenth century, the members living in the host cities usually opened up their homes and provided sleeping arrangements for out-of-town visitors. In such a setting, one individual was known to have 30 guests sleep in his house, and he fed even dozens more than that!

Perhaps the reason this custom does not prevail today is simply because more people are able to afford hotels and restaurants. But there seems to be more to it than that. Could it be that the more money we have, the more aloof we become? Many today would feel it demeaning or intrusive to depend on a host family for food and lodging. Times and customs change, but the requirement to be hospitable never goes away. How can we put Peter's challenge into practice today? —J. B. N.

D. Serving (vv. 10, 11)

10. As every man hath received the gift, even so minister the same one to another, as good stewards of the manifold grace of God.

The community of faith is made up of all kinds of people. That diversity is part of God's plan, so that His people can be equipped to do all kinds of service. We are different by design and are differently empowered by God's Spirit (1 Corinthians 12:12-31). From this perspective, those differences are gifts, the consequence of God's grace for each of His people.

The point of such gifts is that they are to be used in loving, self-giving service for others. To *minister . . . one to another* is simply to serve, providing useful benefits for others that reflect the way that God has generously served and blessed us. This kind of behavior is an exercise of stewardship, meaning responsible management of the resources that God has given to His people. Primary among those resources is God's saving grace, which reminds us that our service is not based on others' deserving it, but on the favor that God has shown us even though we are undeserving.

It is no accident that Peter discusses this as he reminds the readers of the nearness of Christ's return. Jesus told parables about servants who were left with a stewardship to perform in their master's absence. He used the stories to illustrate the faithful service expected from those awaiting His return (Matthew 24:45-47). A church that is faithfully awaiting Christ's return is one in which each Christian exercises his or her distinct gifts to demonstrate God's love to others (Romans 12:6-8).

11. If any man speak, let him speak as the oracles of God; if any man minister, let him do it as of the ability which God giveth: that God in all things may be glorified through Jesus Christ, to whom be praise and dominion for ever and ever. Amen.

Peter now uses two specific examples to illustrate selfless service in the exercise of gifts. Some may be gifted by God to speak. Although they could speak all kinds of things, the grace of God compels them to speak God's Word for the benefit of others. Similarly, the one who is gifted to minister, or to serve practically, should do so to the full extent that God enables, not holding back for selfish reasons.

The readers should see the pattern in these examples and apply them to the exercise of their own distinct gifts. Whatever it is we can do, God's grace compels us to do it in God's service, for the benefit of others, and with the generous measure by which God has given to us.

The result of such service is God's glory. Christians demonstrate to the world who God really is when we serve with self-sacrificial energy and a focus on others. We reflect what God did for us through Jesus when we serve this way. Thus Peter fittingly ends this section with a prayer that Christ receive the praise and power that are rightfully His.

What Do You Think?

Which spiritual gifts do you think you have? How will you better put these into practice?

Talking Points for Your Discussion

- Romans 12:6-8
- 1 Corinthians 12:7-10
- Ephesians 4:11

Conclusion

A. Past, Present, and Future

It is often said that the Christian life is lived in three tenses: past, present, and future. In the past, God saved us through Jesus' death and resurrection. In the present, our sins are forgiven and our lives are being transformed. In the future, Christ will come for His people and establish His rule among them fully and forever. The past and the future shape our present, Peter reminds us. Together, they demonstrate who we are: God's people, bought with the blood of Jesus Christ.

B. Prayer

God Almighty, we reflect with amazement on what You have done for us. You have filled our greatest need. You transform us to fulfill Your highest purpose. We offer our lives to You in service that reflects Your glory. In Jesus' name, amen.

C. Thought to Remember

Live as if you belong to Christ—because you do.

Involvement Learning

Some of the activities below are also found in the helpful student book, Adult Bible Class. *Don't forget to download the free reproducible page from www.standardlesson.com to enhance your lesson!*

Into the Lesson

Mount several large poster boards on different walls of the classroom. Each poster should have the heading *My Favorite Team.* As learners enter, distribute marker pens and say, "Please go to a poster and write the name of your favorite team from any sport. Also sketch something that represents that team (logo, mascot, etc.)." Ask for explanations as appropriate.

Make the transition to Bible study by saying, "When someone dresses in clothing that bears the colors and logo of his or her favorite sports team, observers know the loyalties of that individual. Some Christians even wear clothing with Christian sayings and emblems to show their allegiance to Jesus. However, there is a better way to show our Christian identity."

Into the Word

Early in the week, ask a class member to play the part of Peter for an interview. Give him a copy of the lesson commentary and the questions below in advance. Ideally, your actor should wear a Bible-times costume; if that is not available, he can wear a very large name tag.

Summarize the Lesson Background, then introduce "Peter." Ask the following interview questions, pausing for responses: 1. "Peter, thank you for coming. We're glad you're here to help us know how to live consistently with our identity as Christians. Let me start by asking, did you really cut off the ear of the servant of the high priest?" *(See John 18:10. Peter's embarrassed response may describe the setting, his intent to cut off more than an ear, his subsequent denial of Jesus, etc.)* 2. "Peter, you really have grown in Christ since that day! So when you tell us in verse 1 to 'arm yourselves,' I'm sure you mean something other than a sword. Would you clarify what you mean?" 3. "How can we resist the temptation to fall back into our previous sins?" 4. "In verse 6 you mention that the gospel was preached to those who are dead. Can you clarify?" 5. "Since the end of all things is near, what tips can you give us for living expectantly?" Lead a round of applause for "Peter" as the interview concludes.

Ask learners to work in pairs or trios. Prepare slips of paper with the following topics and Scripture texts, one each. Give one slip to each team: (1) *mind-set,* 1 Peter 4:1, 2, 7; (2) *sex,* 1 Peter 4:2-4; (3) *God's judgment,* 1 Peter 4:5, 6; (4) *prayer,* 1 Peter 4:7; (5) *love,* 1 Peter 4:8, 9; (6) *serving others,* 1 Peter 4:10, 11. Have this printed on each strip: "What are people's attitudes and actions toward your subject while they are unbelievers? How should the attitudes and actions change after accepting Christ?" Ask teams to share conclusions with the class.

Switch to a "big picture" view as you say, "Peter tells us that the end of all things is near. How does remembering that fact help you do a better job of living in a way that glorifies God?"

Alternative: In place of either of the above activities, distribute copies of the "Living as a Disciple" activity from the reproducible page, which you can download. Have learners work in small groups then share discoveries with the class.

Into Life

Say, "First Peter 4:3 lists several things the early Christians needed to give up or otherwise resist as they grew in their new faith." Then pose the following discussion questions: 1. What have you had to change, give up, etc., to make room for spiritual activities or the cultivation of Christian virtues? 2. How has the trade-off been worth it? 3. What behavior or value do you think the Lord still wants you to change or strengthen? 4. How will you make this change? *Option:* Put these questions on a handout for study pairs to consider.

Alternative: Use instead the "Still Growing!" fill-in prayer activity from the reproducible page. This can also be a take-home exercise.

Patient Hope

Devotional Reading: John 14:1-7
Background Scripture: 2 Peter 3

2 Peter 3:3-15a, 18

3 Knowing this first, that there shall come in the last days scoffers, walking after their own lusts,

4 And saying, Where is the promise of his coming? for since the fathers fell asleep, all things continue as they were from the beginning of the creation.

5 For this they willingly are ignorant of, that by the word of God the heavens were of old, and the earth standing out of the water and in the water:

6 Whereby the world that then was, being overflowed with water, perished:

7 But the heavens and the earth, which are now, by the same word are kept in store, reserved unto fire against the day of judgment and perdition of ungodly men.

8 But, beloved, be not ignorant of this one thing, that one day is with the Lord as a thousand years, and a thousand years as one day.

9 The Lord is not slack concerning his promise, as some men count slackness; but is longsuffering to us-ward, not willing that any should perish, but that all should come to repentance.

10 But the day of the Lord will come as a thief in the night; in the which the heavens shall pass away with a great noise, and the elements shall melt with fervent heat, the earth also and the works that are therein shall be burned up.

11 Seeing then that all these things shall be dissolved, what manner of persons ought ye to be in all holy conversation and godliness,

12 Looking for and hasting unto the coming of the day of God, wherein the heavens being on fire shall be dissolved, and the elements shall melt with fervent heat?

13 Nevertheless we, according to his promise, look for new heavens and a new earth, wherein dwelleth righteousness.

14 Wherefore, beloved, seeing that ye look for such things, be diligent that ye may be found of him in peace, without spot, and blameless.

15a And account that the longsuffering of our Lord is salvation.

. . . .

18 But grow in grace, and in the knowledge of our Lord and Saviour Jesus Christ. To him be glory both now and for ever. Amen.

Key Verse

The Lord is not slack concerning his promise, as some men count slackness; but is longsuffering to us-ward, not willing that any should perish, but that all should come to repentance. —**2 Peter 3:9**

Undying Hope

Unit 3: A Call to Holy Living

Lessons 10–13

Lesson Aims

After participating in this lesson, each student will be able to:

1. Describe the argument of the scoffers and how Peter answers them.
2. Explain how the promise of Christ's return should inspire faithful patience in believers.
3. Write a letter to encourage a hypothetical young believer who is discouraged about the apparent hopelessness of winning the lost or about the apparent delay in Christ's return.

Lesson Outline

Introduction
- A. Distance and Perspective
- B. Lesson Background

I. Scoffers' Perspective (2 Peter 3:3, 4)
- A. What They Do (v. 3)
  - *Skepticism, Proper and Improper*
- B. What They Say (v. 4)

II. History's Perspective (2 Peter 3:5-7)
- A. Destroyed by Water (vv. 5, 6)
- B. Destroyed by Fire (v. 7)

III. God's Perspective (2 Peter 3:8, 9)
- A. His Timetable (v. 8)
- B. His Patience (v. 9)

IV. Believers' Perspective (2 Peter 3:10-15a, 18)
- A. Future Event (vv. 10-13)
- B. Present Response (vv. 14, 15a, 18)
  - *Two Kingdoms*

Conclusion
- A. Patient Endurance
- B. Prayer
- C. Thought to Remember

Introduction

A. Distance and Perspective

Judging distance is a tricky business. It is often a matter of perspective. For example, mountain peaks may appear to be very close together if viewed from a distance. But if we fly over the mountains in an airplane, we may see that they are, in fact, widely separated.

The passing of time can also be a matter of perspective. When we are young, time seems to drag on forever. Just a few weeks in school feels like an eternity. But as more time passes, the more quickly it seems to pass. Adults commonly ask themselves "Where did the time go?" as they think back across decades.

So how does time appear from God's perspective? That question underlies today's study.

B. Lesson Background

Today's lesson brings us again to 2 Peter, the great apostle's letter of final instructions before his impending death (see the Lesson Background to Lesson 11). By the time of the letter's writing, a generation had passed since the resurrection of Jesus. The faith had spread widely. Churches had been established all over the eastern part of the Roman Empire, and the Christian movement had become controversial. Christianity was the object of curiosity, ridicule, and even persecution.

At the heart of the controversy was the declaration that Jesus, who had been crucified by the Romans, had not only risen from the dead but now reigned as king at God's right hand. He would one day return to establish His rule fully and finally. That belief challenged the way that many Jewish people understood how God would send the promised king, whom they expected to appear as a military and political ruler. It challenged the Roman Empire's claim to absolute authority, as a man crucified by the Romans as a criminal was declared to be king.

The idea that Jesus would return to establish His rule fully, ending this present age and ushering in a new Heaven and earth, disturbed the widely held notion that the world would continue forever. The promise of Christ's return was challenged on another front as well. Years had passed since Jesus' death and resurrection. Why had He not returned, as His followers said He would? His people appeared to be forgotten, abandoned, or—worst of all—mistaken and misled. What were the believers of the latter half of the first century AD to make of this difficult issue? Today's lesson confronts this problem head-on.

I. Scoffers' Perspective

(2 Peter 3:3, 4)

A. What They Do (v. 3)

3. Knowing this first, that there shall come in the last days scoffers, walking after their own lusts.

Peter's warning focuses on activity *in the last days* (compare Jude 18). While that may sound to us as if such a period of time still lies in the future, the context shows that Peter understands the problem he is describing to be present already. From the perspective of the New Testament, the last days began with the appearance of Jesus, especially with His death and resurrection (compare Hebrews 1:2). Jesus inaugurated the last days when He came as the fulfillment of God's end-time promises.

Because the last days represent the climax of God's saving activity, they also represent the climax of opposition to God's plan (compare 1 John 2:18). So in the last days the faithful can expect to experience intense opposition to their faith, as the forces of the enemy try to frustrate God's program.

That is Peter's implication here: the last-days battle is going on already. The opposition is led by people who are driven by their own selfish desires instead of devotion to God. They ridicule and mock sacred ideas, hoping to discredit them so that they can remain free to do as they wish.

HOW TO SAY IT

Habakkuk	Huh-*back*-kuk.
Noah	*No*-uh.
patriarchs	*pay*-tree-arks.
Thessalonians	*Thess*-uh-***lo***-nee-unz (*th* as in *thin*).

Skepticism, Proper and Improper

It seems that scoffers have always been with us. Almost every technological innovation has been met with skepticism at first. When John Ericsson first proposed the ironclad *Monitor* during America's Civil War, many said it would not even float, much less be a useful warship. When the Wright brothers built their first airplane, many said it would never get off the ground. The list is endless.

Scoffers find it hard to accept anything that is not within their own experience. When I was a youngster in the 1950s, we spent Saturday mornings watching space travel with Buck Rogers on TV. We knew it was all science fiction—with a big emphasis on the *fiction* part. Little did we know that we eventually would put a man on the moon. No reasonable person scoffs about this now.

But it's not always wrong to be a skeptic. Jesus teaches us to be skeptical of various claims concerning His return (Mark 13:32; Luke 17:22-24). William Miller predicted Jesus' return for 1843; Charles Taze Russell predicted it for 1914; Edgar Whisenant wrote a pamphlet, "88 Reasons Why the Rapture Could Be in 1988"; Harold Camping predicted it twice for 2011. Skepticism of these predictions turned out to be well founded! Even so, we are confident that Christ will come again because that is what He promised. —J. B. N.

B. What They Say (v. 4)

4. And saying, Where is the promise of his coming? for since the fathers fell asleep, all things continue as they were from the beginning of the creation.

Here we clearly see that Peter is addressing a situation that is already present in his own time. A generation has passed since Jesus arose and the gospel went forth. Christians have proclaimed repeatedly Jesus' coming as being near. But 30-plus years seems a long time, enough for skeptics to call into question the church's belief in Jesus' return.

The sarcastic rhetoric of the skeptics is captured here. "Today is just like every other day since the beginning of time," they say. "The ancient patriarchs, long dead, would see nothing different today from then. There is no change so far, so we should expect no change in the future."

From the impatient perspective of selfish humanity, three decades seems to be more than enough time to show that the promise of Christ's return is empty. Yet in holding this perspective, the skeptics are ignoring certain evidence, as we see next.

What Do You Think?

How do you respond to unbelievers who laugh at the false predictions of Christ's return?

Talking Points for Your Discussion

- Person-to-person responses
- Responses in a group setting

II. History's Perspective

(2 Peter 3:5-7)

A. Destroyed by Water (vv. 5, 6)

5. For this they willingly are ignorant of, that by the word of God the heavens were of old, and the earth standing out of the water and in the water.

Peter will not allow the mockery of the scoffers to stand. When they affirm that "all things continue as they were from the beginning of the creation" (v. 4), they should realize that the very fact of creation is itself a witness to change.

The earth standing out of the water echoes the description of God's action in Genesis 1:6-10. This demonstration of God's power begins to make Peter's case. Since the world exists because God called it into existence, then God has the power to call it out of existence as well. Since the world began in this way, it is not at all reasonable to assume that it will go on forever. Its continued existence is subject to the will of its Creator.

What Do You Think?

What challenges you most in keeping a historical perspective? How do you overcome this?

Talking Points for Your Discussion

- "The tyranny of the urgent"
- "History is more or less bunk" (Henry Ford)
- A focus on "what works"
- Other

6. Whereby the world that then was, being overflowed with water, perished.

The account of the great flood in Genesis 6–8 is the illustration ready at hand that shows God's power to destroy what He created (compare 2 Peter 2:5). God can and will do with His creation what He chooses to do. This should give pause to anyone who mocks the idea of Christ's return. This is also an additional challenge to the skeptics' claim that "all things continue as they were from the beginning of the creation."

B. Destroyed by Fire (v. 7)

7. But the heavens and the earth, which are now, by the same word are kept in store, reserved unto fire against the day of judgment and perdition of ungodly men.

Having looked back in biblical history, Peter now looks toward what we might call "future history." God preserves the world presently for the judgment that He will bring in the future. That one will not be with flood waters, but with fire. That event will mean God's guilty verdict *(judgment)* and ruin *(perdition)* on all those who, like the scoffers of Peter's day, reject Him to follow their own selfish desires.

III. God's Perspective

(2 Peter 3:8, 9)

A. His Timetable (v. 8)

8. But, beloved, be not ignorant of this one thing, that one day is with the Lord as a thousand years, and a thousand years as one day.

The perspective now shifts from past and future history to the throne room of the eternal God. God's existence is not bound by time as is ours. Because He exists without beginning or ending, the passing of time is to God not the problem that it is for us. "Soon" on God's calendar is not a matter of days, but of great epochs.

The scoffers have failed to reckon with this reality. God's timetable may be very different from our own. What seems like forever to us is insignificant to the God who has existed forever (compare Psalm 90:4).

The failure to grasp this perspective betrays human self-centeredness. We tend to judge everything by our own experience. In a human lifetime,

30 years is a long time. From God's perspective, though, it is not. The same is true for 2,000 years or for any finite number of years we may imagine.

What Do You Think?

How has your perspective on time changed through the years? How has this affected the way you face various issues?

Talking Points for Your Discussion

- Regarding financial issues
- Regarding possessions
- Regarding priorities
- Regarding relationships
- Regarding health concerns
- Other

B. His Patience (v. 9)

9. The Lord is not slack concerning his promise, as some men count slackness; but is longsuffering to us-ward, not willing that any should perish, but that all should come to repentance.

Granted that the passing of time is different from God's perspective, the scoffer could still ask why God bothers to delay the return of Christ at all. Certainly, God may not find the time significant, but why bother at all to leave a period of time between Christ's resurrection and the establishment of His full reign? Why not begin the final judgment immediately, if indeed there is to be such a thing?

Peter's reply to such an objection is vital to our understanding of God's dealings with the world. It expresses the implication of God's essential nature. God is just; therefore, He must bring judgment on evil. But God is also merciful, wanting to forgive those who have committed evil. So in His mercy, God withholds judgment while He invites rebellious humans to accept His offer of forgiveness and be reconciled to Him. Without a delay between Christ's resurrection and His return, no such opportunity would exist.

So, says Peter, God has in no way been late or neglectful in fulfilling His promises. In fact, He is faithfully fulfilling His promise to save by allowing sinful humans time to hear His gracious offer in the gospel and come to Jesus in repentance. This is an expression of God's patience as He pursues His profound desire to bring all people to repentance and reconciliation, if only they are willing (compare 1 Timothy 2:4).

From God's perspective, this is no delay at all (compare Habakkuk 2:3). He is working out His plan to bring as many people as possible into an eternal relationship with Him. From the beginning, God has advanced His plan by which His enemies can become His friends. The seeming postponement of Christ's return is another step in that plan, allowing more rebellious humans to accept His terms of mercy.

IV. Believers' Perspective

(2 Peter 3:10-15a, 18)

A. Future Event (vv. 10-13)

10a. But the day of the Lord will come as a thief in the night;

The perspective now shifts to what faithful believers know about Christ's return and how they will be affected. The Lord's return as *a thief in the night* echoes Jesus' own words in Matthew 24:42-44 and Luke 12:39, 40 (compare 1 Thessalonians 5:2, 4 [Lesson 8]; Revelation 16:15). For those who reject the gospel and do not expect Christ's return, His coming will be a disastrous surprise.

The outcome will be different for believers. We expect Christ's return, and we will welcome Him when He arrives. For the scoffer, He returns with judgment; for the believer, He returns with blessing.

10b. In the which the heavens shall pass away with a great noise, and the elements shall melt with fervent heat, the earth also and the works that are therein shall be burned up.

The description now shifts to the fate of the universe as a whole: it *shall melt with fervent heat.* The world that the scoffer takes to be eternally unchanging, the place where the scoffer puts confidence and hope, will be destroyed. This includes *the works that are therein*—the things people have made, which they count as sources of security and power. Every pretension of humanity will come to nothing when Christ returns. For those who do not know Him as Savior, His coming means the destruction of what they think will save them.

11. Seeing then that all these things shall be dissolved, what manner of persons ought ye to be in all holy conversation and godliness?

For the believer, the knowledge that Christ will one day destroy this present existence has transformative power. We realize that there is no basis for security in the things of this present age. Relying on power or status on the world's terms is foolish because the world has no staying power.

Instead, what matters is *holy conversation and godliness*. The word *conversation* means not just speech, but all kinds of proper interaction with others. A life of *godliness* speaks to proper devotion to the true, eternal God. Our confident hope for the future demands that we live with an eternal perspective every day.

12. Looking for and hasting unto the coming of the day of God, wherein the heavens being on fire shall be dissolved, and the elements shall melt with fervent heat?

Unlike the scoffer, the Christian lives in expectation of Christ's return. The expression *looking for* implies "watching expectantly." We can compare this with children who look out the window waiting for a parent to arrive home after work.

The phrase *hasting unto the coming of the day of God* is difficult. Taken literally, it could mean that we somehow are able to "speed up" the timetable of Christ's return. Taken figuratively, the phrase carries the idea of "waiting eagerly" for that return. Such waiting is not passive, but involves applying energy and enthusiasm to obeying the Lord in anticipation of His return. As we do, we sit lightly on the things of this present age, knowing that such things are marked for destruction.

Visual for Lesson 13. *Pose the question on this visual when your study reaches verse 13. Allow a time of sharing of responses.*

13. Nevertheless we, according to his promise, look for new heavens and a new earth, wherein dwelleth righteousness.

The Christian's perspective is to be defined by Christ's promises. Thus importance is placed not on the world that is passing away, but on the one to come.

The description that Peter provides is important, and we ought to pay careful attention to the language. First, we must remember that the combination "heavens and earth" is based on Old Testament usage, as in Genesis 1:1. As such, "heavens and earth" refers to the entirety of God's creation.

This causes us to realize that what Peter describes is not the destruction only of the earth so that the heavens remain. Rather, what is in view is the replacement of this present realm with a new one, *new heavens and a new earth.*

The new heavens and earth will be characterized by righteousness. In this new sphere, God's will shall be done perfectly. This is the promise of the Old Testament prophets (Isaiah 65:17; 66:22), renewed here and in the closing chapters of the New Testament (Revelation 21:1).

B. Present Response (vv. 14, 15a, 18)

14. Wherefore, beloved, seeing that ye look for such things, be diligent that ye may be found of him in peace, without spot, and blameless.

If our destination is a righteous world, the way we live in the present should reflect that destination. Considering the scope of Christ's return, our duty in the present is clear. We are like servants whose master is away: we want to be found doing His work when He returns (Luke 12:35-40).

As servants of Christ, we therefore pursue what He taught, namely true purity that exists inside and out, being spotless and blameless even where only the Lord himself can see—in our minds and hearts. Likewise, we pursue peaceful, positive relationships with others, just as Christ commanded. Servants with this kind of life will be commended by their master at His return.

What Do You Think?

If you knew there was a 50/50 chance of Christ returning tomorrow, how would you change your approach to *godliness* today?

Talking Points for Your Discussion

- Dealing with unrepentant sin
- Asking forgiveness from others
- Extending forgiveness to others
- Other

Two Kingdoms

An influential doctrine of Martin Luther (1483–1546) was his teaching of the two kingdoms. We live in a world governed by earthly authorities, authorities that God instituted (Romans 13:1, 2). At the same time, we live in a kingdom not of this world, a kingdom governed directly by God. The tricky part is to live responsibly in both at the same time so that we do not disregard one in favor of a total emphasis on the other.

Living in both kingdoms means we are to be heavenly minded (Colossians 3:1, 2) while also being salt and light in this world (Matthew 5:13-16). Peter was certainly aware of the fleeting nature of earthly existence. But this did not cause him to treat our earthly existence lightly; we see quite the opposite attitude as he encouraged his readers to live "in peace, without spot, and blameless."

The two kingdoms need not be in conflict, but a Christian certainly needs to know which one is the higher calling. We demonstrate that awareness in the way we live. —J. B. N.

15a. And account that the longsuffering of our Lord is salvation.

In the meantime, we may become impatient for the Lord's return. When life is difficult, we will long for Christ to return and put an end to the evil that we suffer. But if we understand the perspective that Peter shares, we will view the wait for Christ's return as God views it: an expression of God's patience. He waits for more people to return to Him. So we wait along with God himself, with our focus being what His focus is: bringing others to reconciliation with Him.

18. But grow in grace, and in the knowledge of our Lord and Saviour Jesus Christ. To him be glory both now and for ever. Amen.

After a brief discussion regarding how the apostle Paul also affirms these truths (vv. 15b-17, not in today's text), Peter turns to a closing word of encouragement. Knowing that Christ will indeed return compels that we continue in the gifts we have received from Him. We *grow in grace* as we respond consistently to God's unmerited gift of salvation. We *grow . . . in the knowledge* as we put into practice what we have learned through the gospel. By these means Christ is glorified.

What Do You Think?

Where do you need to grow most in Christ as you await His return? How will you do so?

Talking Points for Your Discussion

- Growth in grace (John 1:14-17; 2 Corinthians 1:12; Ephesians 4:7; Hebrews 13:9; James 4:6; etc.)
- Growth in knowledge (Romans 1:28; Ephesians 4:13; Philippians 1:9; Colossians 1:10; etc.)

Conclusion

A. Patient Endurance

How do we respond to the reality of Christ's expected return? We may be reluctant to desire His return when we feel comfortable; we may be anxious for His return when we are suffering. Whatever our circumstances, we need to recognize how important to our faith is the promise of His return to save and to judge. Remembering this promise will strengthen the patient endurance we need to stand firm and grow in our faith in a hostile world.

B. Prayer

Father, may Your Son return quickly! But if He tarries, we know it is so that more may be saved. Make us the agents of that reconciliation as You give us the strength to wait. In Jesus' name, amen.

C. Thought to Remember

"Behold, I come quickly; and my reward is with me" (Revelation 22:12).

INVOLVEMENT LEARNING

Some of the activities below are also found in the helpful student book, Adult Bible Class.
Don't forget to download the free reproducible page from www.standardlesson.com to enhance your lesson!

Into the Lesson

Form four teams of no more than five learners each. Give each team several Christian songbooks and/or hymnals. Say, "Select a song that speaks of the second coming of Christ. The reference may be in the song as a whole or in a specific line or verse." Ask teams to share their selections and reasons for choosing them. Say, "Christian music anticipates and celebrates Jesus' second coming. We must always remember that He will come again!"

Into the Word

Read the printed text, then assign the following four passages of Scripture to the same four groups above, one each: 2 Peter 3:3-7; 2 Peter 3:8, 9; 2 Peter 3:10-13; and 2 Peter 3:14, 15, 18. (*Option:* Depending on the nature of your class, you may wish to provide copies of the lesson commentary for the verses assigned.)

Ask each group to create an artistic depiction that represents or interprets its passage. They may choose a drawing, clay sculpture, new song lyric to an existing tune, or poetry. For example, a team may choose to write an additional verse to the children's song "Jesus Loves Me" to express truths of the passage. Make available sheets of poster board or paper, marker pens, colored pencils, modeling clay, and Christian songbooks or hymnals. Allow no more than 15 minutes for this creative activity.

After teams share results with the class, say, "Artistic representations of Scripture can be emotionally uplifting! But we also want to wrestle with the text mentally."

Distribute copies of the following questions to the same four teams, one set per team as numbered. Each team will have two questions to explore and answer for the class. *Team 1*—verses 3-7: What argument is given by the "scoffers"? How does Peter use creation and the flood to answer their argument? *Team 2*—verses 8, 9: How is God's perspective on time different from ours? What important reason does Peter give for God's apparent delay in fulfilling His promise? *Team 3*—verses 10-13: What facts does Peter give about what "the day of the Lord" will be like? How should Christians act in light of these facts? *Team 4*—verses 14, 15, 18: As we await Christ's return, what can we do in the meantime? What comfort and encouragement does Peter give to Christians who are suffering?

Alternative: If you choose not to do the artistic depiction exercise above, you can follow the text examination exercise with the "What We Need to Have" activity from the reproducible page, which you can download. Distribute copies for the four teams to complete as a closed-Bible exercise.

Into Life

The next activity may be done as a whole class or in the teams that have been working together through the lesson thus far. Read the following situation, then distribute handouts with the same wording:

> *One of your coworkers has been experiencing extreme hardship for two years. The problems began when she went through a difficult divorce, losing custody of her children to their father. Living on a very limited income from her secretarial work, she has been hammered by bills for car repairs and a mistake she made on her income tax return. This past week she discovered she will need surgery. You have become very concerned about the possibility that she will take her own life when you heard her say, "I just don't want to be here anymore. I have nothing to live for."*
>
> *You have invited her for lunch to talk and provide support. Using today's passage of Scripture as a foundation for your discussion, what can you say to her, without being flippant, to encourage perseverance?*

Alternative: Instead of the above, distribute copies of the "Living in Hope" exercise from the reproducible page. After allowing a few minutes for personal reflection, ask volunteers to share thoughts.